CAMBRIDGE

MORE!

2ⁿᵈ Edition 1

Herbert Puchta & Jeff Stranks
G. Gerngross C. Holzmann P. Lewis-Jones

HELBLING
LANGUAGES

Student's Book

Grammar	Vocabulary and Pronunciation	Skills and Communication	**MORE!**
STARTER Welcome back!			
• subject pronouns • present simple of *be* • possessive adjectives • plural nouns	• classroom objects and language • greetings • saying hello • numbers • asking about age • international words • colours • days of the week Sounds right the alphabet	• listen to and understand international words • listen to and complete a dialogue to introduce yourself • read about other people and where they are from • listen to and complete facts about other people • spelling • talk about yourself and others	
UNIT 1 How are you?			
• subject pronouns (revision) • present simple of *be* (revision) • questions with *Who* (revision) • possessive adjectives (revision)	• feelings • numbers (1-20) (revision) Sounds right days of the week (revision)	• introduce yourself • ask how people feel • ask about age • read, talk and write about days of the week and feelings • listen and order a dialogue • complete a form	**Culture** The United Kingdom **Extra Reading** International Crime Busters Europe: London
UNIT 2 Where's your book?			
• prepositions of place • questions with *Who, Where, Why, What, What colour?* • imperatives	• classroom objects • prepositions of place Sounds right /ə/	• ask and say where things are • give instructions • ask for words in English • read about classrooms around the world • listen to a description of classroom objects • ask and answer about classroom objects • write a description of a friend	**The Story of the Stones 1 DVD** They're here! **CLIL** Maths: graphs and charts **Check your progress 1** Units 1 and 2
UNIT 3 Your house is fantastic!			
• *there is/are* • questions with *Whose...?* and the possessive *'s* • adjectives	• adjectives • furniture • rooms	• describe things • give information • describe rooms and furniture • listen to a description of a room • read and talk about your ideal bedroom • write a description of your ideal bedroom	**Culture** Houses around the world **Extra Reading** International Crime Busters Europe: Berlin
UNIT 4 Is he French?			
• *have got* • the article *a / an*	• parts of the body • countries and nationalities • describe people Sounds right /h/	• talk about nationality • describe people • talk about possessions • read descriptions of people • listen to and understand descriptions of people • describe famous people • write a profile for your best friend	**The Story of the Stones 2 DVD** Don't worry - it's me! **CLIL** Geography: continents and nationalities **Check your progress 2** Units 3 and 4
UNIT 5 I never eat chips!			
• present simple (positive) • spelling: 3rd person singular • adverbs of frequency	• food • in a restaurant Sounds right /ɪ/ and /iː/	• reply to offers • talk about favourite foods • listen and talk about what you eat • read about different diets and foods • write about what you eat	**Culture** School in England **Extra Reading** International Crime Busters Europe: Athens

Grammar	Vocabulary and Pronunciation	Skills and Communication	MORE!

UNIT 6 I go to bed at ten

Grammar	Vocabulary and Pronunciation	Skills and Communication	MORE!
• present simple (negatives and questions and short answers) • object pronouns	• daily activities **Sounds right** days of the week chant (revision)	• ask and tell the time • talk about routines / times • read about other people's daily routines • listen and talk about daily routines • write about your day	**The Story of the Stones 3 DVD** Don't be scared! **CLIL** Science: a healthy diet **Check your progress 3** Units 5 and 6

UNIT 7 How much is this?

Grammar	Vocabulary and Pronunciation	Skills and Communication	MORE!
• demonstrative adjectives and pronouns • countable and uncountable nouns • *How much? / How many?* • *some / any*	• clothes	• talk about prices • talk about and describe clothes • buy clothes in a shop • listen, read and understand a story • invent the ending to a story • write a text about unusual clothes	**Culture** Sports in Great Britain **Extra Reading** International Crime Busters Europe: Madrid

UNIT 8 I love singing!

Grammar	Vocabulary and Pronunciation	Skills and Communication	MORE!
• *can* for ability / permission • *can* questions and short answers • *like / love / hate doing*	• family members **Sounds right** *can*	• talk about ability • ask for permission • talk about things you like doing • talk about family • read a text about an acrobat • listen and understand what activities people do • talk about fitness • write a text about sports	**The Story of the Stones 4 DVD** Rats! **CLIL** Music: the orchestra **Check your progress 4** Units 7 and 8

UNIT 9 Where are you calling from?

Grammar	Vocabulary and Pronunciation	Skills and Communication	MORE!
• present continuous	• telephone numbers • ordinal numbers • months of the year • dates	• talk on the phone • talk about birthdays • discuss dates • say what people are doing • read about mobile phones • listen and understand a phone conversation • write a postcard	**Culture** TV or not TV? **Extra Reading** International Crime Busters Europe: Zurich

UNIT 10 I'm surfing the web!

Grammar	Vocabulary and Pronunciation	Skills and Communication	MORE!
• articles • present simple vs. present continuous	• computers • free-time activities **Sounds right** /w/	• make invitations • talk about your free time • listen and talk about technology • read about collections • write about a hobby	**The Story of the Stones 5 DVD** Two more to go! **CLIL** Technology: mobiles **Check your progress 5** Units 9 and 10

UNIT 11 The chocolates were delicious!

Grammar	Vocabulary and Pronunciation	Skills and Communication	MORE!
• past simple of *be* (positive, negative, questions and short answers) • past time expressions	• furniture • prepositions (revision) **Sounds right** *was / were*	• say where people were • say where things are / were • read, listen to and understand a mystery story • talk and write about the past	**Culture** British history **Extra Reading** International Crime Busters Europe: Norway

UNIT 12 Where were you last night?

Grammar	Vocabulary and Pronunciation	Skills and Communication	MORE!
• past simple	• things to do • places to go **Sounds right** /t/ /d/ /ɪd/	• say when you were somewhere • find out information • read and listen to a story • write a short letter	**The Story of the Stones 6 DVD** Three stones to rule the universe! **CLIL** History: biography **Check your progress 6** Units 11 and 12

Vocabulary The classroom

02 CD1

1 Look at the picture. Write the numbers in the boxes. Listen and check.

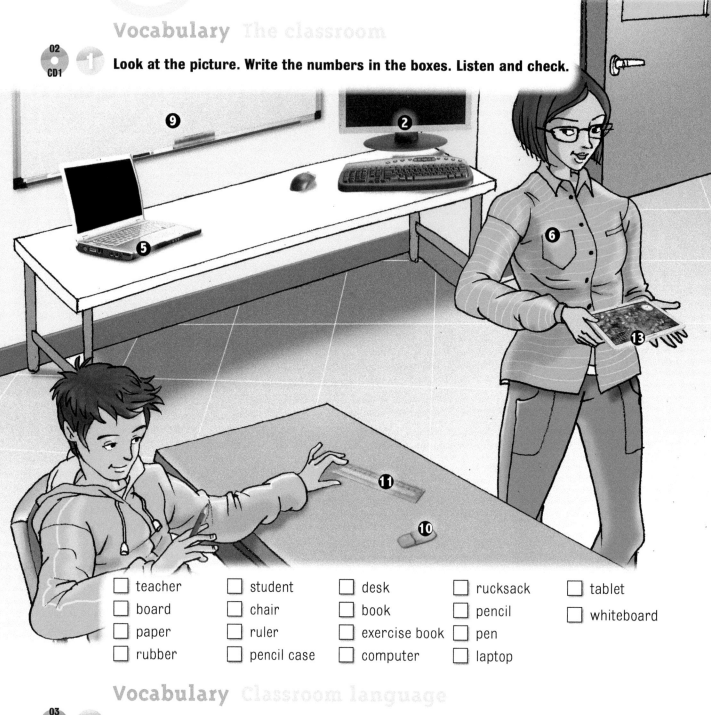

☐ teacher	☐ student	☐ desk	☐ rucksack	☐ tablet
☐ board	☐ chair	☐ book	☐ pencil	☐ whiteboard
☐ paper	☐ ruler	☐ exercise book	☐ pen	
☐ rubber	☐ pencil case	☐ computer	☐ laptop	

Vocabulary Classroom language

03 CD1

2 a Listen and repeat.

b Write S next to the phrases for students and T next to the ones for the teacher.

I don't understand. ....

Look at the board. ....

Copy the sentence. ....

Can you repeat that, please? ....

Listen to the CD. ....

Do exercise four, please. ....

What's the homework, please? ....

Sorry, I'm late. ....

How do you spell 'ruler'? ....

Vocabulary

Greetings

  Listen and repeat.

Luke	Bye, Mum!
Mum	Goodbye, Luke.

Mrs Jones	Good morning, Luke.
Luke	Good morning, Mrs Jones.

Luke	Hello, Jenny.
Jenny	Hi, Luke.

Luke	Good afternoon, Mrs Smith.
Mrs Smith	Good afternoon, Luke.

Newsreader	Good evening.
Mum	Goodnight, Luke.
Luke	Goodnight, Mum.

4 Work in pairs. Practise the dialogues. Change the names and invent new ones.

Saying hello

  Listen and repeat.

Michela	Hi Sue! How are you?
Sue	Hi, Michela. I'm fine. And you?
Michela	Great, thanks!

Ahmed	Hello, Matt! How are you?
Matt	I'm fine. How are you, Ahmed?
Ahmed	I'm fine, thanks!

6 Work in pairs and practise the dialogues. Change the names and invent new ones.

Communication

Asking about age

 06 CD1

 7 Listen and repeat. Write the words.

six
eight
seventeen
twelve
fifteen
~~two~~

1 **2** **3** **4** **5** **6** **7**

one ....two........ three four five .... seven

8 **9** **10** **11** **12** **13** **14**

.... nine ten eleven .... thirteen fourteen

15 **16** **17** **18** **19** **20** **21**

.... sixteen .... eighteen nineteen twenty twenty-one

 07 CD1

 8 Listen and circle the correct names and numbers.

A Hi! What's your name?
B I'm *Sarah / Susie*.
A How old are you?
B I'm *13 / 14*.

C Hi! What's your name?
D I'm *Tom / Tim*.
C How old are you?
D I'm *13 / 14*.

 9 Work in pairs. Practise the dialogues. Change the names and ages and invent new ones.

Grammar

Simple present of *be* Positive

Subject pronouns	*be*	
I	am	
He / She / It	is	14.
You / We / They	are	

10 Circle the correct verb.

1 He *is / am / are* nine.
2 It *is / am / are* great.
3 I *am / is / are* thirteen.
4 She *is / am / are* fourteen.

5 We *are / is / am* students.
6 You *are / is / am* a teacher.
7 They *are / is / am* exercise books.

Subject pronouns

11 Listen and read. Circle the subject pronouns below.

Hi, I'm Jenny.
This is Sally. She is my friend.
This is Mark. He is my friend too.
They are my best friends.
We are students at Gateways School.
It is a great school.

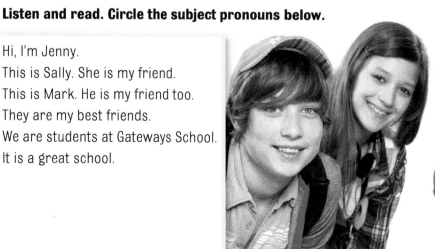

Grammar

12 Complete the dialogue with the correct subject pronouns.

I
you
he
she
it
we
you
they

❶ Hi, ...'m Holly.

❷ This is Amy. .... is my friend.

❸ And this is Jake. .... is my friend too.

❹ .... are my best friends.

❺ .... are students at Summerville School.

❻ ....'s a great school.

13 Complete the text for yourself. Then tell the class.

Hi, I'm ....
This is .... is my friend.
And this is .... is my friend too.
We are students at .... school.

Plural nouns

To make nouns plural, we add an '**s**'.

14 Reread the text in exercise 12 and complete the table.

Singular	Plural
friend	1.................................
student	2.................................
teacher	teachers

Some plurals are irregular:

Singular	Plural
child	children
man	men
woman	women
person	people

15 Make the sentences plural.

1 The ruler is blue.
The rulers are blue..........................

2 The child is 14.
....

3 The pen is red.
....

4 The man is English.
....

5 My friend is great.
....

6 The book is about London.
....

Grammar

Possessive adjectives

Subject pronoun	Possessive adjective
I	my
He / She / It	his / her / its
You / We / They	your / our / their

16 **Listen and read. Use the table above. Circle the possessive adjectives in the text.**

Hi! My name is David and this is my family.

My dad – his name is Alan.

My mum – her name is Christina.

Our surname is Spencer.

And the fish? Their names are Splish and Splash!

And the car? Its name is Betty.

What's your name?

17 **Complete the sentences with the correct possessive adjective.**

1
2
3
4

1 .... name is Cristiano.

2 .... name is Mila.

3 .... names are Robert and Kristen.

4 .... name is *The Batmobile*.

5 What's your name?
.... name is ....

6 What's the name / number of your class?
.... class is ....

18 **Complete the sentences about yourself and your family. Use the words below.**

my
our
her
your
his

¹.............. name is ....

This is my mum. ².............. name is ....

This is my dad. ³.............. name is ....

⁴.............. surname is ....

What's ⁵.. surname?

Skills

Vocabulary Days of the week

19 **Complete the days of the week. Then listen and repeat.**

M _ _ D A _	**F R _ _ A Y**
T _ E _ D _ Y	**S _ T _ _ D A _**
W E _ _ E S _ A _	**S _ _ D _ Y**
T _ U _ _ D A _	

20 **Answer the question. Then ask six friends. Write their names in the diary above.**

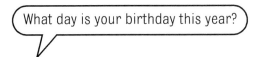

What day is your birthday this year?

Vocabulary Colours

11
CD1

21 **Write the colours under the correct picture. Then listen, check and repeat.**

grey   red   green   blue   yellow   orange   pink   purple   black   white

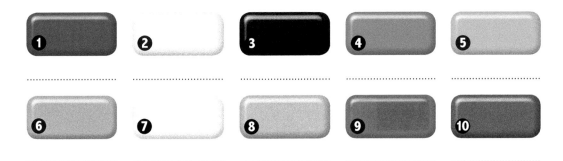

1   **2**   **3**   **4**   **5**

6   **7**   **8**   **9**   **10**

12
CD1

22 **Listen and repeat. Ask other students about their favourite colour.**

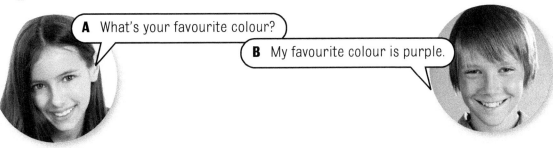

A What's your favourite colour?

B My favourite colour is purple.

Skills

International words

 13 CD1 23 **Write the words under the pictures. Listen and check.**

bus
tennis
hotel
taxi
hamburger
pizza
football
supermarket

1 ....   2 ....   3 ....   4 ....

5 ....   6 ....   7 ....   8 ....

Sounds right The alphabet

 14 CD1 24 **Listen and repeat the alphabet.**

A	B	C	D	E	F	G
H	I	J	K	L	M
N	O	P	Q	R	S	T
U	V	W	X	Y	Z

 15 CD1 25 **Listen and circle the correct letter.**

Spelling

 16 CD1 26 **a Listen and repeat.**

A How do you spell 'hotel'?
B H-o-t-e-l / I don't know.

C How do you spell your name?
D M - A - R - I - O

b Work with a partner. Choose different words and names. Ask and answer about spelling.

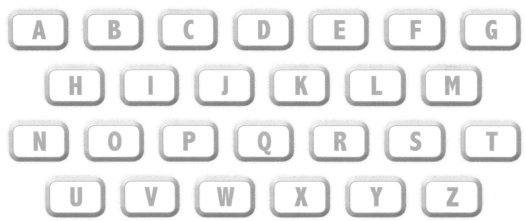

12 STARTER

Skills

Reading

 Read the texts and complete the table below.

Hi, my name's Michael. I'm from London. I'm twelve years old and I'm in Year 8 at school. My favourite colour is red. My favourite food is pizza.

Hi, my name's Alice. I'm from Brighton. I'm thirteen years old and I'm in Year 9 at school. My favourite colour is purple. My favourite food is chicken.

NAME		
FROM		
AGE		
YEAR		
FAVOURITE COLOUR		
FAVOURITE FOOD		

Listening

 17 CD1 **Listen and complete the dialogue.**

Jake What's your [1].................................. ?

Sarah My name's Sarah.

Jake How old are you?

Sarah I'm [2].................................. years old.

Jake Where are you from?

Sarah I'm from [3].................................. .

Jake What's your favourite colour?

Sarah My favourite colour is [4].................................. .

Jake And what's your favourite food?

Sarah My favourite food is [5].................................. .

Writing and speaking

 Complete the dialogue for yourself. Then practise it with a friend.

You learn
- subject pronouns (revision)
- present simple of *be* (revision)
- questions with *Who?*
- possessive adjectives (revision)
- words for feelings
- numbers (revision)

and then you can
- introduce yourself
- ask how people feel

18
CD1

1 Listen and read.

Kelly	Hi, Joe, hi, Adam!
Joe, Adam	Hello, Kelly!
Kelly	How are you?
Joe	Fine, thanks.
Adam	And you?
Kelly	I'm OK. This is Leah. She's new.
Joe	Hi, Leah!
Leah	Hi. Are you Joe?
Adam	No, my name's Adam. And this is Joe.

Joe	Nice to meet you.
Kelly	Come on, Leah. We're late for Meg's party.
Adam	Oh, a party? Who's Meg?
Leah	My sister. She's eight today.
Joe	Mmm – a party! With cake … I'm hungry!
Kelly	Sorry, boys. It isn't for you! Guests only! Bye!
Leah	See you!

Dialogue work

2 Write the names under the pictures.

Kelly
Joe
~~Adam~~
Leah

① *Adam* **②** **③** **④**

3 Write the names in the spaces.

1 .... is fine.
2 .... is new.
3 .... is OK.

4 .... is eight today.
5 .... is hungry.

Introducing yourself

4 Listen and complete the dialogues.

Dialogue 1

Olivia Hello, Emma. How are you?
Emma Hi, Olivia. I'm fine, thanks.
        How ¹.............. you?
Olivia Great, thanks.
Emma Olivia, this ².............. Lucas.
Lucas Hi, Olivia. Nice to meet you.
Olivia Hi, Lucas. Nice to meet you too.

Dialogue 2

Noah Hi, Tom. Meet Anna and Kim.
        They ³.............. new here.
Kim Hi, Tom!
Tom Hi, Kim and Anna. Oh, sorry.
        I ⁴.............. late. Bye!
Kim and Anna Bye, Tom.
Noah Bye, bye!

5 Act out the dialogues from exercise 4.

Vocabulary

Feelings

1

a Listen and circle the correct word.

Lucas **David** **Peter** **Kate**

1 angry/bored   2 excited/sad   3 tired/hungry   4 bored/cold

James **Grace** **Tina** **Anna** **Sarah** **Fred**

5 hot/scared   6 angry/sad   7 hot/cold   8 sad/happy   9 nervous/hungry   10 angry/worried

b Now work with a partner and ask and answer.

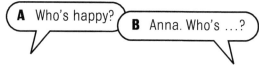

A Who's happy?   **B** Anna. Who's …?

Numbers (revision)

2

a Listen and circle the correct numbers.

1 *three / nineteen* books
2 *six / sixteen* pens
3 *thirteen / fifteen* pencils
4 *twenty / four* houses

5 *nine / nineteen* chairs
6 *eleven / eighteen* friends
7 *twelve / twenty* students
8 *seven / seventeen* computers

b Listen and write the correct numbers.

1 .... taxis
2 .... laptops
3 .... friends
4 .... books

5 .... footballs
6 .... pencils
7 .... buses
8 .... pens

Sounds right Days of the week (revision)

3

a Complete the days of the week. Number them in the correct order.

⚪ Th ....   ① *Monday*
⚪ Su ....   ⚪ F ....
⚪ W ....   ⚪ Tu ....
⚪ Sa ....

b Listen and check.

Communication

Asking how people feel

4 **Listen and match the names and the feelings.**

1 Anna ☐	a angry
2 Fred ☐	b worried
3 Lucas ☐	c hot
4 Tina ☐	d happy
5 Peter ☐	e nervous
6 David ☐	f sad
7 Kate ☐	g hungry
8 Grace ☐	h scared
9 James ☐	i bored
10 Sarah ☐	j cold
11 Mike ☐	k tired

5 **a** **Now interview four of your classmates.**

A How are you today?

B I'm *happy / OK / sad.*

b **Report back to the class.**

Anna is happy today but David is sad.

Sarah is happy today and Joe is too.

Asking about age

6 **Work in pairs. Ask and answer questions about the photos.**

A How old is *Mike*?

B He's *twelve.*

A *That's right. / That's wrong – he's …*

MIKE 12

JANE 17

SIMON 15

JACKIE 16

ERICA 11

TOM 14

Grammar

Subject pronouns (revision)

All English sentences need a subject and a verb.

Look at the dialogue on page 14 and complete the examples with the correct subject pronouns.

¹........'m hungry. ²........'s new. ³........'re late.

I'm Patrick.   **It**'s new.

You're in class 2A.   **We**'re friends.

He's seven.   **You**'re hungry.

She's happy.   **They**'re angry.

1 **Circle the correct subject pronoun.**

1 *He / I / They* are from London.
2 *It / You / We* is nice.
3 *I / You / They* am thirteen.
4 *We / They / She* is fourteen.
5 *I / He / We* are English.

2 **Complete the sentences with the correct pronoun.**

.... are excited!

.... is a teacher.

.... are twenty.

.... am late.

.... are scared.

.... is a nice car.

.... is from London.

Present simple of *be* Positive (revision)

I'm (= I **am**) sad.

You're (= You **are**) cold.

He's (= He **is**) bored.

She's (= She **is**) in class 3B.

It's (= It **is**) blue.

We're (= We **are**) busy.

You're (= You **are**) happy.

They're (= They **are**) twelve.

3 **Complete the text with *am*, *is* or *are*.**

1 Hi, I'm Elina and I ¹.............. thirteen now. My pencil case ².............. blue. This is my friend, Bobby. He ³.............. from Manchester. We ⁴.............. in Year 8 at school.

2 Hello! I'm Shelly and this is Dean. We ⁵.............. in Year 7. Look at our bags! They ⁶.............. purple. Purple is our favourite colour!

Present simple of *be* Negative

Look at the dialogue on page 14 and complete the example.

It ¹........... for you!

I'm not nervous. (= I am not …)

You / We / They **aren't** happy.
(= You / We / They are not …)

He / She / It **isn't** hungry.
(= He / She / It is not …)

4 **Circle the correct word.**

1 He *isn't / aren't* happy today.
2 They *isn't / aren't* hungry.
3 It *isn't / aren't* Sunday – it's Monday!
4 I *isn't / 'm not* hungry.
5 You *isn't / aren't* cold.
6 We *isn't / aren't* scared.

Grammar

 Present simple of *be* **Questions and short answers**

Complete the questions with *Am*, *Is* **or** *Are*.

Questions

¹.......... I right?

Are you happy?

².......... Sally nervous?

Is it Monday?

Are we late?

³.......... Fred and Dan hot?

Short answers

Yes, you are. / No, you aren't.

Yes, I am. / No, I'm not.

Yes, he / she is. /
No, he / she isn't.

Yes, it is. / No, it isn't.

Yes, you are. / No, you aren't.

Yes, they are. / No, they aren't.

5 **Complete the questions with the correct word.**

1 .... you happy?

2 .... he hungry?

3 .... I late?

4 .... they excited?

5 .... we in the correct class?

6 .... it Friday tomorrow?

6 **Now write the answers.**

1 Yes, ...

2 No, ...

3 Yes, ...

4 Yes, ...

5 No, ...

6 Yes, ...

 Questions with *Who?*

Look at the dialogue on page 14 and complete the example.

¹.......... Meg?

To ask about someone, use *Who?*

A Who's (is) he? **B** He's (He is) David.

A Who are they? **B** They're (They are) David and Maria.

7 **Write the questions.**

1 *Who's he* ....? He's Mark.

2 ....? She's Mrs Page.

3 ....? We're the new students.

4 ....? I'm Frances.

5 ....? They're *One Direction*!

 Possessive adjectives (revision)

Dawn is **my / your / her / his / our / their** sister.

I'm the singer in a band. **Its** name is *Be Bop*.

8 **Listen and repeat the rap.**

 25 CD1

Skills

Reading

 Read and tick (✓) the correct pictures.

Monday

It's Monday morning and Kevin's scared. He's got an English test.

It's Tuesday afternoon. Kevin's bored.

It's Wednesday evening. Kevin's hot.

It's Thursday evening. Kevin's angry. He's got a lot of homework.

It's Friday afternoon. Kevin's excited. Tomorrow's Saturday.

It's Saturday. Kevin's very happy.

It's Sunday. Kevin's sad. There's school tomorrow.

Tuesday

 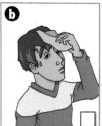

Wednesday

 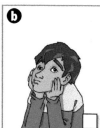

Thursday

Friday

Saturday

 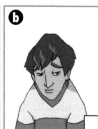

Sunday

Listening and speaking

  a Listen and number the dialogue in the correct order.

- ☐ **A** OK. Here's a slice of pizza.
- ☐ **A** How are you, Julia?
- ☐ **A** Hungry? OK – here's an apple.
- ☐ **B** An apple? Yuk. No, thanks.
- ☐ **B** A slice of pizza! Thanks. Now I'm happy!
- ☐ **B** I'm hungry. I'm really hungry.

b Work in pairs. Practise the dialogue below. Invent new ones.

A How are you, (*name*)?

B *I'm happy. I'm really happy! / I'm worried. I'm really worried.*

A *That's great! / Oh no!*

Skills

Speaking

3 **a** **Look at Dave's diary. Say how he feels.**

On Monday, he's sad.

Monday	☹	History Test!
Tuesday	☺	Football!!
Wednesday	☺	PE this morning!
Thursday	☹	Maths!
Friday	☺	It's the weekend!

b **Now complete the diary below for yourself and discuss in pairs.**

A *On Monday, I'm happy.*
B *Why?*
A *It's school!*

| Monday |
| Tuesday |
| Wednesday |
| Thursday |
| Friday |

Writing Completing forms

4 **a** **Complete the form.**

About me
Name:
Age:
Nationality: *From*
School:
My friends:
I am happy / sad / excited etc today.

Put your photo here!

b **Write a short text about you.**

My name is …………………………… . I'm ………… and I'm from ……………………………
……
……
……
I'm …………………………… today.

CULTURE
The United Kingdom

Look at the map and complete the table.

London Belfast The Bann Ben Nevis Loch Ness Cardiff

	ENGLAND	SCOTLAND	WALES	N. IRELAND
Mountains		1	Snowdon	
Rivers	The Thames	The Tweed		2 ....
Lakes	Windermere	3		
Capital cities	4	Edinburgh	5	6 ....

The facts

COUNTRIES
England, Scotland, Wales and Northern Ireland

LANGUAGES
English, Welsh, Gaelic and Irish

POPULATION
63,002,000

A view over London

Read about London and match the photos to the correct places.

- [ ] The London Eye is the biggest wheel in Europe. It is 135 metres high with 32 capsules for 25 people.

- [ ] Buckingham Palace is the home of the Queen of England. It is big with 600 rooms. There are 400 servants and 39 royal guards here.

- [ ] The Globe Theatre is one of London's most famous theatres and a copy of Shakespeare's Globe Theatre. It is a round theatre with no roof.

- [ ] Covent Garden is a market with shops and stalls and nice clothes and crafts.

MORE! Online Action Box
**Listening and Quiz online.
Write a text for the MORE! Online journal. Put it online for students from other countries to read.**

> Go to www.cambridge.org/elt/more for extra CULTURE

INTERNATIONAL
CRIME BUSTERS
EUROPE

The International Crime Busters are flying into London.

Four robberies in four days. Scotland Yard are worried!

❶

Outside Scotland Yard.

Hello. I'm Nick Diamond, and this is Lucy Pond. We're ICB agents.

Thanks for coming.

❷

The shops are all in the same area.

Yes, they are. I think this is the next one.

❸

JEWELLERY

I think he's inside the shop!

Yes, he is!

❹

JEWELLERY

Look! He's there!

Come on. Let's get him!

❺

That's the back door to Madame Tussauds.

Quick. Let's go and talk to the manager.

❻

Call the police.

And close the doors!

❼

That's the last one. Sorry, but your man isn't in the building.

Hmmm, maybe. He's very clever, isn't he?

❽

Are you sure he's here?

Yes, I am, and I know where!

❾

Good work. So he's the robber!

Yes! Look...Henry VIII with a watch? Impossible!

❿

UNIT 2 Where's your book?

You learn
- prepositions
- questions with *Who, Where, Why, What, What colour?*
- imperatives
- words for classroom objects
- prepositions

and then you can
- say where things are
- give instructions

28
CD1

1 Listen and read.

Mr Jones	Good morning, class!
Class	Good morning, Mr Jones!
Mr Jones	Who's this?
Leah	I'm Leah.
Mr Jones	Ah, yes, Leah - the new girl.
Leah	Yes, that's right!
Mr Jones	I'm Mr Jones, your English teacher. Sit here, Leah, next to Kelly. Take out your books, please. Adam, where's your book?
Adam	It's in my bag, Mr Jones.

Mr Jones	Well, open your bag then!
Adam	But my bag isn't here, Mr Jones.
Mr Jones	Where is it?
Adam	I don't know, Mr Jones.
Mr Jones	Don't laugh, Joe. It isn't funny. What colour is your bag, Adam?
Adam	It's black and white.
Mr Jones	Is that your bag under Joe's chair?
Adam	Yes, it is!
Mr Jones	Joe, give Adam his bag. Be quiet, everyone, and open your books.

Dialogue work

2 **Circle the correct answer.**

1 Leah sits next to *Joe* / *Kelly*.
2 Mr Jones is a *teacher* / *student*.
3 *Joe's* / *Adam's* book isn't on his desk.
4 Adam's bag is black and *red* / *white*.
5 Mr Jones is *happy* / *angry* when the class laughs.
6 Adam's bag is under *Leah's* / *Joe's* chair.

Saying where things are

3 **Work in pairs and make dialogues about school objects.**

A Where's my *rubber*?
B I don't know. What colour is it?
A It's *white*.
B Look! It's there *under your chair*.

Giving instructions

4 **Match the pictures to the speech bubbles and write the correct number.**

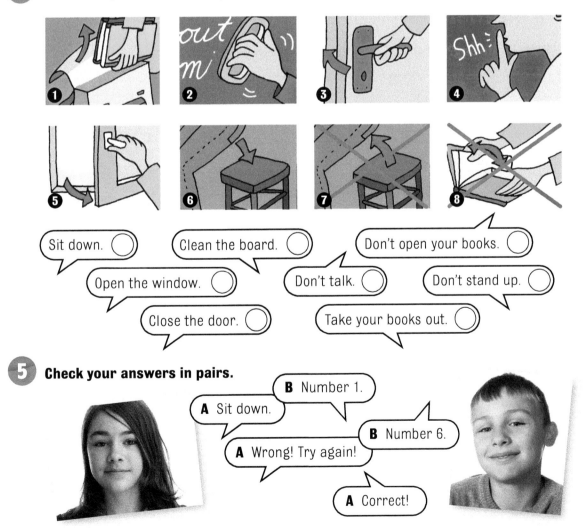

5 **Check your answers in pairs.**

Vocabulary

Classroom objects

1 **Read and label the objects in the picture.**

In my classroom, the floor is grey and our desks are green. Our chairs are orange. The teacher's desk is brown. The door is red. My bag is yellow and pink. Yellow and pink are my favourite colours. My pencil case is blue and my ruler is black.
My rubber is green.

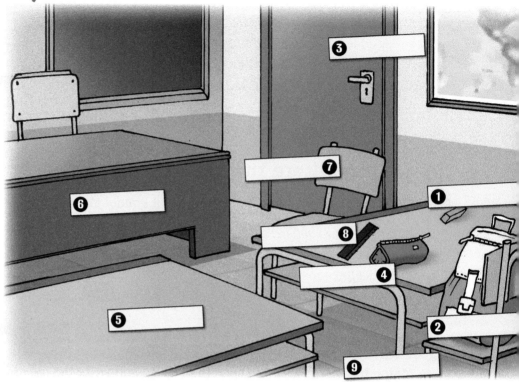

Prepositions of place

2 **Where is the dog? Write the correct preposition under the picture.**

in
on
under
next to
in front of
behind

1 ....

2 ....

3 ....

4 ....

5 ....

6 ....

3 **Work in pairs and talk about different objects in and around the classroom.**

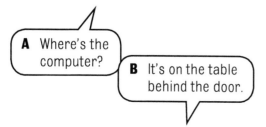

A Where's the computer?

B It's on the table behind the door.

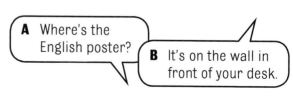

A Where's the English poster?

B It's on the wall in front of your desk.

Communication

Sounds right /ə/

4 **a** **Listen and repeat.**

1 teach**er**   2 comput**er**   3 play**er**   4 und**er**   5 numb**er**   6 col**our**

b **Listen and repeat.**

1 Why is the teacher under the desk?
2 What colour is the teacher's computer?

Asking for words in English

5 **a** **Complete the sentences with the correct word from your language.**

1 What's .... in English? It's 'rucksack'.
2 What's .... in English? It's 'pencil case'.
3 What's .... in English? It's 'rubber'.

b **Work in pairs and ask and answer about other objects in the classroom.**

Saying where things are

6 **Work in pairs. Look at the picture for 1 minute then close your books and ask and answer about the objects in the list below.**

rucksack
pencil case
laptop
computer
bag
books
tablet
TV

A Where's the laptop?

B It's in front of the TV.

A Correct. / No, it's not. It's in front of the window.

Giving instructions

7 **Work in pairs. Tell each other things to do around the classroom.**

A Stand up, please!   **B** Open your book, please!

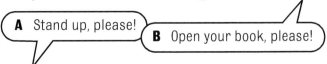

Grammar

Prepositions

1 Write the prepositions under the correct picture.

next to   in   under

¹............   on   ²............   ³............   in front of   behind

2 Complete the text with the words below.

in (x2)   behind   on   next

Hi, my name is Zena. I'm fourteen and I'm
¹..................... class 5A. My desk is ².....................
to the window and my friend Anna's desk is
³..................... my desk. My exercise book is
⁴..................... my desk. My pencils and pens are
⁵..................... my pencil case .

3 Look at the picture and complete the sentences.

in   on   under   next to   on   next to

Look at the chair ¹................................. the
window. There's a dog ²................................. the
chair and a cat ³................................. the chair!
And my school bag is in the corner. There's a
ruler ⁴................................. the bag. My English
book is ⁵................................. the floor,
⁶............................. my bag.

Questions with *Who, Where, Why, What, What colour?*

4 Look at the dialogue on page 24 and complete the table.

¹................... 's your book?

²................... is your bag, Adam?

Who's she?

Why are you under the desk?

What's the capital of Peru?

Translate the question words into your own language.

5 Circle the correct word.

1 *What / Where* is your English teacher's name?
2 *Who / What colour* is your rucksack?
3 *Who / Why* is your best friend?
4 *Where / What* is he from?
5 *Why / What* is he here?
6 *Where / What* is your dog now?

6 Complete the sentences with the correct question word.

1 .... is your name?
2 **A** .... is your pen?
   B It's red.
3 **A** .... is in your class?
   B Sue is.
4 .... is your pencil?
5 .... are you in this class? This is 4D not 4A!
6 .... is the teacher? He's late.

7 Read the answers then complete the questions.

1 .... is my tablet?
   It's on the table next to the window.
2 .... class is he in?
   7A.
3 .... are you with?
   Sarah.
4 .... is the teacher late today?
   She's with the headmaster.

Grammar

Imperatives

8 Look at the dialogue on page 24 and complete the table.

+	−
¹................. here, Leah...	**Don't put** your books in your bag.
²................. out your books, please.	**Don't run**!
³Well, ... your bag then!	⁴................. laugh, Joe.

9 Complete the phrases.

Don't   Clean   Sit   Take   Stand   Close

1 .... out your books.
2 .... the window, please. I'm cold!
3 .... open your books!
4 .... up!
5 .... down!
6 .... the board.

10 Match the sentences from exercise 9 with the pictures. Write the numbers.

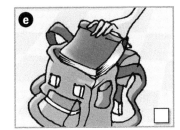

11 Reorder the words and write sentences.

1 the / close / door

....

2 your / books / open

....

3 up / stand / don't

....

4 down / don't / sit

....

5 the / window / open / don't

....

6 open / don't / door / the

....

7 pairs / in / work

....

8 board / clean / the / please

....

Now do CYBER HOMEWORK 2a www.cambridge.org/elt/more

Skills

Reading

1 **a** **Read and match the person to the correct classroom.**

1 Hi, my name's Catalina.

I'm eight years old and I'm from Chile. My classroom is a blue and white bus with desks and chairs and pictures on the walls. It's great! My desk is next to the bus door. My favourite exercise book is orange and my favourite pencil is red and green.

2 Hi, my name's Alhad.

I'm eleven years old and I'm from India. There are mats on the floor in our classroom. My schoolbag is green and my pencil case is yellow. My favourite colours are yellow and green. They are the colours of my favourite football team.

3 Hello, my name's Arro.

I'm ten years old and I'm from Finland. There is a whiteboard in our classroom and the desks are orange with black chairs. My schoolbag is red and my pencil case is black. Our exercise books for English are blue.

b **Answer the questions.**

1 How old is Catalina?
2 Where is her classroom?
3 What colour is her favourite pencil?
4 Who is from India?
5 How old is he?

6 Where are the mats in his classroom?
7 What are his favourite colours?
8 Where is Arro from?
9 What colour is the board in his classroom?
10 What are blue?

Listening

31
CD1

2 **Listen to Ben and tick (✓) the objects he talks about.**

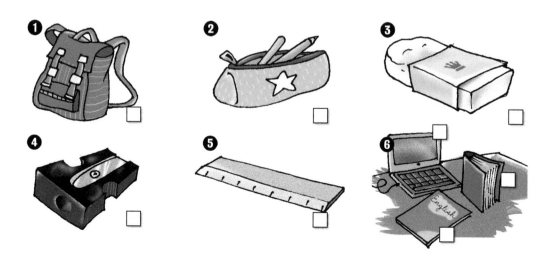

Skills

Speaking

3 Work in pairs. Interview your partner. Then change the words and invent new dialogues.

Boy What colour's your *pencil case*?
Girl It's *blue and green*.
Boy OK. What colour's your *rucksack*?
Girl My *rucksack*? It's *yellow*.
Boy What's your favourite colour?
Girl *Yellow*!

A What colour's your pencil case?

B Blue.

Writing Descriptions

4 **a** Complete the text with the adjectives below.

happy   sad   yellow   brown   green   blue   pink   purple

This is Emma. Her hair is [1].................................... .
Her eyes are [2].................................... .
She is [3].................................... today.
She is not [4].................................... .

This is her rucksack. It is [5].................................... .
Her pencil case is [6].................................... .
Her ruler is [7].................................... . Her favourite colour is [8].................................... .

Tip   Note!

Adjectives always come **after** the verb *be*.

b Now write a description of a friend and his or her schoolbag.

DVD — The Story of the Stones 1   They're here!

Watch Episode 1 and match the pictures to the phrases.

1 Let me see.   **2** How strange!   **3** At last!

Go to www.cambridge.org/elt/more for **DVD** exercises and **CYBER HOMEWORK 2b**

CLIL Maths

Graphs and charts

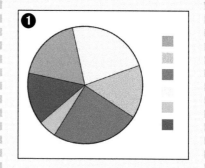

....

1 Read the key facts and label the diagrams.

Key facts!

Data is another word for information.

Data can be shown on graphs and charts.

Here is a pie chart, a bar chart and a line graph.

Which one is which?

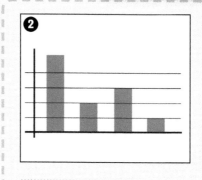

....

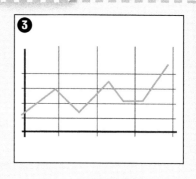

....

2 30 students talk about their favourite colours. Answer the questions below.

1 What is their favourite colour? ....

2 Does anyone like pink? ....

3 Does anyone like black? ....

4 Do more students like purple or green? ....

5 How many colours do they like in total? ....

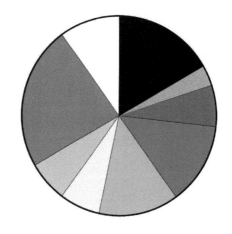

Favourite colours:
- ■ purple
- ☐ white
- ■ green
- ■ black
- ■ blue
- ■ pink
-   yellow
- ■ orange
- ■ red

3 The students make a bar chart to show how they feel. Answer the questions below.

1 Use the chart to find out how many students feel sad. ....

2 How many feel happy? ....

3 How many are excited? ....

4 Do any students feel scared? ....

5 How many students are in the class? ....

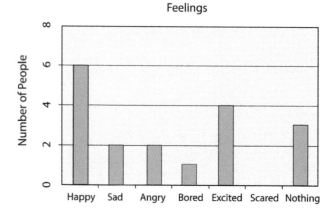

Feelings

WEBQUEST

◢ Draw a graph or a pie chart for the students in your class on a computer. Choose one of the topics from exercise 2 or 3.

◢ Print it out and present it to the class.

Go to www.cambridge.org/elt/more for extra CLIL

Check your progress 1

1 Write the numbers. [½ point each]

seventeen ....

eight ....

thirteen ....

twenty-five ....

twelve ....

fourteen ....

☐ **3**

2 Write the objects.

1 c _ _ _ _   4 CD _ _ _ _ _ _

2 c _ _ _ _ _ _ _   5 d _ _ _

3 b _ _ _ _   6 w _ _ _ _ _

☐ **6**

3 Complete the questions.

1 .... you bored?

2 .... your pen on your desk?

3 .... Steve scared of dogs?

4 .... Sue and John happy?

5 .... your sister 12 years old?

☐ **5**

4 Match the answers to the questions in exercise 3.

a .... No, she's 13.

b .... Yes, I am.

c .... Yes, he is.

d .... Yes, it is.

e .... Yes, they are.

☐ **5**

5 Complete the questions and answers. [2 points each]

1 .... colour is your pencil case?

....

2 .... is your favourite actor?

....

3 .... is your rucksack?

....

4 .... is your English teacher?

....

5 .... is the capital of your country?

....

6 .... old are you?

....

☐ **12**

6 Write the sentences using the negative form.

1 I'm new here.

....

2 They are hungry.

....

3 It's very hot today.

....

4 My teachers are friendly.

....

5 Yellow is her favourite colour.

....

6 We are late for school.

....

☐ **6**

7 Complete the dialogue.

A [1]..................... morning, Mrs Carter.

B Hello, Tim. How [2].....................
[3]..................... ?

A [4]..................... fine, thanks.
This [5]..................... Jane.

B Hi, Jane. Nice [6]..................... meet
[7].....................

☐ **7**

8 Translate the sentences.

1 My pencil is under my desk.

....

2 Our car is in front of the school.

....

3 The cat is on the chair.

....

4 Don't look at your book!

....

5 Sit next to the window.

....

6 Don't be sad!

....

☐ **6**

TOTAL ☐ **50**

MY PROGRESS SO FAR IS... brilliant! ☐   quite good. ☐   not great. ☐

UNIT 3 Your house is fantastic!

You learn
- *There is / are*
- questions with *Whose...?* and the possessive *'s*
- adjectives
- words for furniture
- rooms in the house

and then you can
- describe rooms and furniture
- give information

32 CD1

1 **Listen and read.**

Kelly What's your new house like, Leah?

Leah It's great.

Adam Is it big?

Leah Umm – well, yes, it is. There are six bedrooms and three bathrooms.

Adam Six bedrooms? Wow! Is there a TV in your bedroom?

Leah Yes, there is. And there's a DVD player too, and a computer on the desk.

Kelly Really?

Leah Yes. But there isn't a wardrobe.

Kelly So, where are your clothes?

Leah In the room next to my bedroom.

Adam Your wardrobe is a room?! Wow, your house is fantastic! Are there any good posters on the walls? In your bedroom, I mean.

Leah Of course! There are posters of all my favourite singers and bands. And there are lots of bookshelves, too. But there aren't a lot of books!

Kelly Wow. What an amazing house. Can we come and see it?

Leah Sure! You can see it now. Look. There it is.

Kelly But that isn't a big house ... Whose is it?

Adam It's Leah's house! It's a joke!

Leah You're right! It's my house. It isn't big really. There are two bedrooms and a bathroom. There's a desk in my room and posters on the wall, but no computer or TV. And there isn't a garden. But that's OK. We're happy!

Dialogue work

2 **Read the dialogue again and write *Yes* or *No*.**

1 Is Leah's new house big? *No.*
2 Are there six bedrooms? ....
3 Is there one bathroom? ....
4 Are there posters on the walls? ....

5 Is there a desk? ....
6 Is there a computer in Leah's room? ....
7 Is there a garden? ....
8 Is Leah happy in her house? ....

Describing things

3 **a Work with a partner. Find the opposites.**

big   early   friendly   good   old   beautiful   unfriendly   bad   new   ugly   small   late

b Complete the questionnaire for yourself then ask and answer with a partner.

A What's your bedroom like?

B It's small with a window.

What's he/she/it like?	Me	My partner
your bedroom	....	....
your mobile phone	....	....
your house / flat	....	....
your parent's car	....	....
your computer	....	....
your best friend	....	....

Giving information

33 CD1

4 **Complete the dialogue with the words below. Listen and check, then practise it with a partner.**

where
accident
please
spell
fire
in

A Quickly! There's a ¹.................................... in Horton Street!

B Can you ².................................... that, please?

A Yes, it's H-O-R-T-O-N Street.

B OK, an ³.................................... in Horton Street.

A No, there isn't an accident there! There's a fire!

B OK, sorry! And ⁴.................................... are you now?

A I'm ⁵.................................... Winchester Street.

B Can you spell that too, ⁶.................................... ?

A W-I-N-C-H-E-S-T-E-R Street! OK?

B OK.

Vocabulary

Furniture and rooms

34 CD1

1 Write the correct number for the rooms and furniture in the list below, then listen and check.

- ☐ kitchen
- ☐ hall
- ☐ living room
- ☐ garage
- ☐ toilet

- ☐ bathroom
- ☐ bedroom
- ☐ bed
- ☐ sofa
- ☐ stereo

- ☐ washbasin
- ☐ bath
- ☐ cooker
- ☐ fridge
- ☐ wardrobe

- ☐ desk
- ☐ armchair
- ☐ cupboard
- ☐ table
- ☐ TV

- ☐ curtains
- ☐ cushion
- ☐ rug
- ☐ bookcase
- ☐ chair

2 Work in pairs. Cover up the list in exercise 1. Your partner says a number. You say the word.

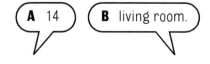

A 14   **B** living room.

Communication

Describing rooms and furniture

3 **Work in pairs. Describe one of the rooms in exercise 1. Your partner guesses which one it is.**

> **A** There's a purple sofa and pink cushions.

> **B** It's the living room.

4 **Now describe your house or flat to your partner.**

> There are four rooms in my house / flat, a kitchen, bathroom, etc.

5 **Look at the picture and complete the text with the correct words.**

This is my [1]....................... . There is a really comfortable [2]...................... and next to it, a bedside [3]...................... with a [4]...................... on it. In front of the window, there's a [5]...................... and a [6]...................... . I do my homework at the [7]...................... . My [8]...................... is blue. It's my favourite colour. The [9]...................... and the [10]...................... are blue.

6 **Circle the correct words then check your answers with a partner.**

A What's your bedroom like?

B Well, there's a blue [1]*cooker / rug* and white curtains.

A Is there an armchair?

B No, there isn't, but there's a [2]*sink / chair* by my desk. It isn't an armchair. What about yours?

A Well, there's an armchair and a TV in my [3]*sofa / bedroom*.

B What colour's your armchair?

A It's green, the same as my bed. But the [4]*rug / bath* is blue and yellow.

B My bed's blue – the same as the rug. I like blue!

7 **Practise the dialogue in exercise 6 with a partner then use it to describe your bedroom at home.**

8 **Work with partner. Talk about your favourite rooms.**

> **A** What's your favourite room in your house?

> **B** It's the living room because it's big with red and yellow curtains.

Grammar

There is/are

1 **Look at the dialogue on page 34 and complete the table below.**

Positive	Negative	Questions	Positive	Negative
There is a nice big wardrobe.	² .... a wardrobe.	³ .... a TV in your bedroom?	Yes, ⁵	No, there isn't.
¹ .... six bedrooms and three bathrooms.	There aren't curtains.	⁴ .... any good posters on the walls?	Yes, there are.	No, there aren't.

2 **Circle *There is* or *There are*.**

1 *There is / There are* a poster of a horse in my room.
2 *There are / There is* two blue chairs in the room.
3 *There is / There are* a computer on the table.
4 *There is / There are* a pencil case on the floor.
5 *There are / There is* six books in the room.
6 *There are / There is* twenty children in the class.

3 **Put the words into the correct order and write sentences.**

1 bag / a / the / in / book / is / There / .
....

2 are / bags / the / There / floor / on / three / .
....

3 in / the / white / living room / There / are / curtains / .
....

4 a stereo / There / in / is / room / my / .
....

5 armchair / in / red / the / There / hall / a / is / .
....

6 in / two / are / garage / the / There / cars / .
....

4 **Write a description of the room in the photo.**

....
....
....
....
....
....
....
....
....
....
....

Grammar

Questions with *Whose...?* and the possessive *'s*

5 Look at the dialogue on page 34 and complete the table below.

Use **Whose..?** to ask who something belongs to:

¹........................ is it? It's Leah's house.

Bob**'s** dog. (This is Bob. This is his dog.)

Nigella**'s** pizza.(This is Nigella. This is her pizza.)

6 Rewrite the sentences. Use the names of the people in brackets with the possessive *'s*.

1 Is it her desk? (Sandra)
Is it Sandra's desk?

2 This MP3 player is hers. (Lucy)
....

3 It's his pen. (Tim)
....

4 It's her cat. (Martha)
....

5 Steak is his favourite food. (Ken)
....

6 They're her CDs. (Sandy)
....

7 What's her favourite colour? (Annie)
....

8 Where's her schoolbag? (Jane)
....

9 Is this his? (Mike)
....

10 Are they his pictures? (Tom)
....

7 Follow the lines and write sentences using the possessive *'s*.

Meg   Noel   Sarah   Ben   Sue   David

1 Whose smartphone is it?
It's Meg's.

2 Whose camera is it?
....

3 Whose books are they?
....

4 Whose rucksack is it?
....

5 Whose desk is it?
....

6 Whose tablet is it?
....

Skills

Listening

1 **a** **Listen and circle the recycled objects in the picture below.**

Recycled Rooms!

	Object
bicycle	....
wood from garden	....
dad's old jackets	....
old bottles	....
old suitcase and cushion	....

b **Now complete the table. Write the name of the recycled objects.**

Speaking

2 **What is your ideal bedroom like? Tick the items below then interview your partner.**

	Me	My partner
big	☐	☐
desk	☐	☐
posters and photos	☐	☐
sofa	☐	☐
curtains	☐	☐
photos	☐	☐
cupboards	☐	☐
rug	☐	☐
TV	☐	☐
computer	☐	☐
DVD player	☐	☐
wardrobe	☐	☐
bookcase	☐	☐

A Is there a sofa?

B Yes there is.

A What colour is it?

A Is it big or small?

A Where is it?

A Are there any posters?

B No, there aren't.

Skills

Reading

3 **Read the description of Hannah's bedroom and circle T (True) or F (False).**

My bedroom is fantastic!

There are five photos of my friends in frames on the wall and there is a small green armchair with red and green cushions. The material for the cushions is my mum's old curtains!! There are two big red cushions on the floor and a small white rug. There is a wooden desk with my computer on it and there are two big bookcases for all my books and CDs.

1 There are three photos on the wall.	**T / F**
2 There is a red armchair with cushions.	**T / F**
3 There is a TV.	**T / F**
4 There are two big cushions on the floor.	**T / F**
5 There is a blue rug on the floor.	**T / F**
6 There are two bookcases.	**T / F**

Writing Order of adjectives

Tip   Remember!

Number	size/shape	colour	object(s)
two	big	blue	picture frames

4 **a Complete the text with the words on the left.**

isn't
is
films
books
cushions
bed
sofa
bedroom

In my ideal ¹.. , there ².. a big TV so
I can watch my favourite ³... There are lots of
⁴.., but there ⁵.. a computer. There is a nice red
⁶.. with five big ⁷... There is a small blue
⁸.. and blue curtains.

b Now write a description of your ideal bedroom.

In my ideal bedroom, there is a ....
There are .... on the wall and ....
on the floor. ....
....
....

Now do CYBER HOMEWORK 3b www.cambridge.org/elt/more

Culture

a

Houses around the world

b

c

Read the texts and match them to the correct photo.

☐ The Mongolian people are from central Asia. They are 'nomads' – they move to find food for their sheep. Their houses are 'yurts'. They are made of wood and felt. Yurts are easy to move. Camels or yaks carry parts of the yurt on their back. There is only one room in a yurt. You can build a yurt in about two hours.

☐ This is a house in Vietnam. It has got long legs – 'stilts'. The house isn't on the ground because there is a lot of rain here. The kitchen is usually in the middle of the house. The family sit and talk there. Sheep, pigs or cows often live under the house.

☐ The Uros people are from Lake Titicaca in Peru. There are about two thousand of them on fifty floating islands of long grass (reeds). Some Uros families have motor boats and solar panels. There is also a floating radio station! The reed is very important to the Uros – they eat it, make tea from it and use it as a medicine.

☐ The Ndebele women are from South Africa. Their houses have bright colours and geometrical designs. Every woman has her own designs and teaches them to her daughters. The designs can have a message - someone in the house is getting married, for example. The women work for a long time to finish their designs.

d

Complete the sentences.

1 There .... about fifty floating islands on Lake Titicaca.
2 The designs on the Ndebele houses sometimes have a ....
3 The Vietnamese house is on stilts because there is a lot of ....
4 A yurt isn't very big - there is only one ....
5 The .... is in the middle of the Vietnamese house.
6 Camels carry the yurts .... their back.
7 The Ndebele are .... South Africa.
8 Some Uros people have .... panels.

MORE! Online Action Box

Listening and Quiz online.
Write a text for the MORE! Online journal. **Put it online for students from other countries to read.**

▸ Go to www.cambridge.org/elt/more for extra CULTURE

INTERNATIONAL CRIME BUSTERS EUROPE

The International Crime Busters are flying into Berlin.

So tell me about this case.

A lot of dogs are missing in Berlin.

1

Fifty dogs in the last month. And all of them are expensive dogs...

And are there any clues at all?

None. I'm sorry. You are on your own.

2

This case is very strange.

Annual Berlin Dog Show

Umm. This is interesting. Maybe we should start here.

3

It's terrible. Only one man with his dog.

And who is this man?

Doctor Wolfgang. His dog, Lucky, was second in last year's show.

Let's talk to this Doctor Wolfgang.

4

Outside Doctor Wolfgang's house.

That's a lot of noise for one dog.

Let's have a closer look.

5

Back at the dog show.

And the winner of best dog is Doctor Wolfgang.

Yes, Lucky. Finally the trophy is ours.

6

Not so fast, Doctor.

Who are these kids? Take them away.

7

8

Dr Wolfgang has the missing dogs! He wanted Lucky to win the show.

Good work, Crime Busters.

9

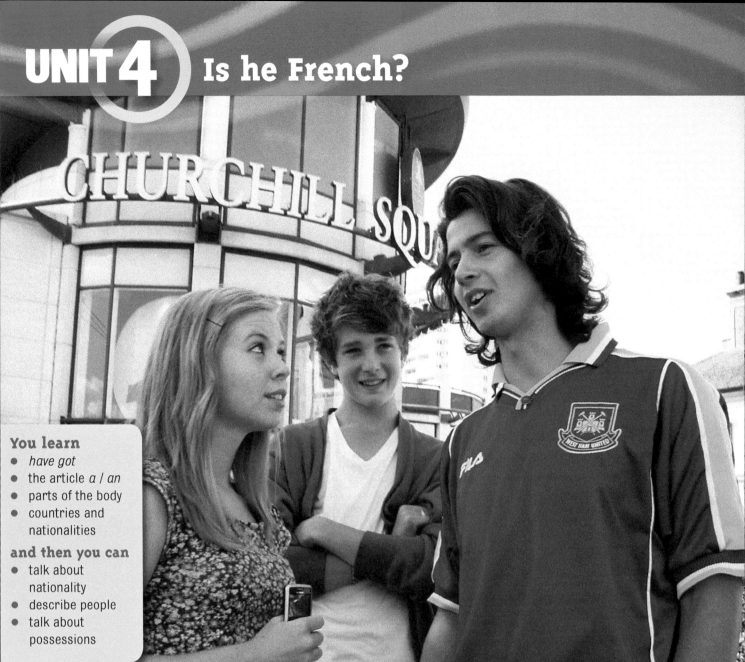

You learn
- *have got*
- the article *a / an*
- parts of the body
- countries and nationalities

and then you can
- talk about nationality
- describe people
- talk about possessions

37 CD1

1 **Listen and read.**

Kelly Who's that?

Joe I don't know. There are lots of people around him.

Kelly He's probably famous … Maybe he's a football star. He's tall, and he's got dark hair and blue eyes.

Joe Has he got a football shirt?

Kelly Yes, he has.

Joe Oh, it's Jerome Brunel. He's the new football player.

Kelly Is he French?

Joe Yes, he is. Take a photo!

Kelly But I haven't got a camera on my phone. It's an old one.

Joe There's a camera on my phone. Go and stand next to him.

(after the photo)

Kelly Thank you, Jerome!

Dave My name isn't Jerome! It's Dave.

Kelly What? Aren't you the famous football player?

Dave No, I'm not! I've got the team's shirt, because they're my favourite team!

Dialogue work

2 Read the dialogue again and correct the mistakes in the sentences below.

1 Dave has got blonde hair.   ....
2 His eyes are brown.   ....
3 He's short.   ....
4 He's got a basketball shirt.   ....
5 Kelly's got a camera.   ....

Talking about nationalities

38
CD1

3 Match the flags to the nationalities, then listen and check.

❶ Jamaica   **❷** France   **❸** Brazil   **❹** Switzerland   **❺** The USA

❻ Turkey   **❼** China   **❽** Italy   **❾** Sweden   **❿** Britain

a Brazilian ☐   d American ☐   g Swiss   ☐   i Jamaican ☐
b Chinese   ☐   e Swedish   ☐   h Turkish ☐   j Italian   ☐
c British   ☐   f French   ☐

4 Look at the photos of these Olympic Champions and say where you think each person is from.

A Where's number *1* from?
B I think *she's from Britain. She's British.*
A *That's right! / That's wrong!*

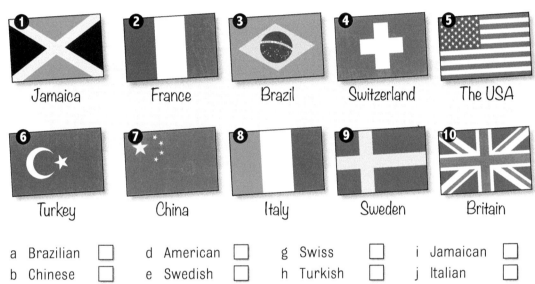

5 Work in pairs. Think of some other famous sportspeople and describe them.

A *He's tall, and he's got fair hair and blue eyes.*   **B** *Is it ... ?*
B *Is he British?*   **A** *Yes, it is. / No, it isn't.*
A *I think so. / No, he isn't. He's ... .*

Vocabulary

Parts of the body

39 CD1

1 Look at the picture and circle the correct labels. Listen and check.

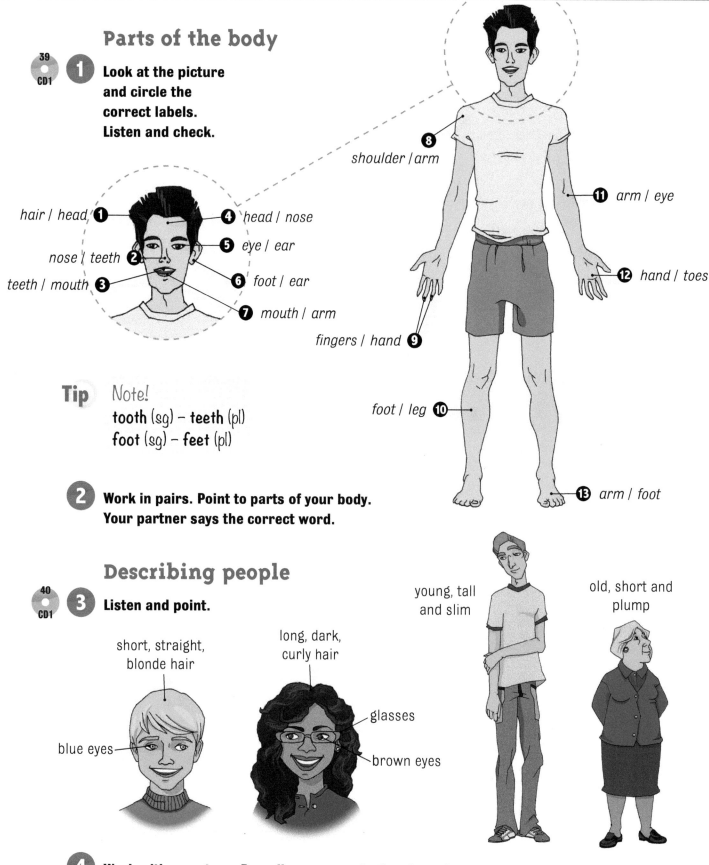

shoulder / arm **8**

11 arm / eye

hair / head **1**
4 head / nose

nose / teeth **2**
5 eye / ear

teeth / mouth **3**
6 foot / ear

7 mouth / arm

12 hand / toes

fingers / hand **9**

foot / leg **10**

13 arm / foot

Tip *Note!*
tooth (sg) – **teeth** (pl)
foot (sg) – **feet** (pl)

2 Work in pairs. Point to parts of your body. Your partner says the correct word.

Describing people

40 CD1

3 Listen and point.

short, straight, blonde hair

long, dark, curly hair

young, tall and slim

old, short and plump

blue eyes

glasses

brown eyes

4 Work with a partner. Describe someone in the class. Guess who it is.

A *He's tall with glasses. He's got short, curly hair.*
B *It's Jorge.*
A *Yes, it is. / No, it isn't. Try again!*

Communication

Sounds right /h/

5 **a** **Listen and repeat.**

1 **h**and   2 **h**appy   3 **h**ead   4 **h**ungry   5 **h**air   6 **h**er

b 1 Put your hands on your head.
2 Is he happy or hungry?

Describing people

6 **a** **Work in pairs. Listen and repeat.**

A Has *Tom* got *blue eyes*?   **A** Has *Maria* got *dark hair*?
B Yes, he has.   **B** No, *she* hasn't. *She's* got *blonde hair*.

b **Now talk about other students in your class.**

A Has *Mario* got *blue eyes*?
B No, *he* hasn't. *He's* got *brown eyes*. / *I don't know*.

Talking about possessions

7 **Interview three other students in your class about possessions and tick the things they have got. Then tell the class.**

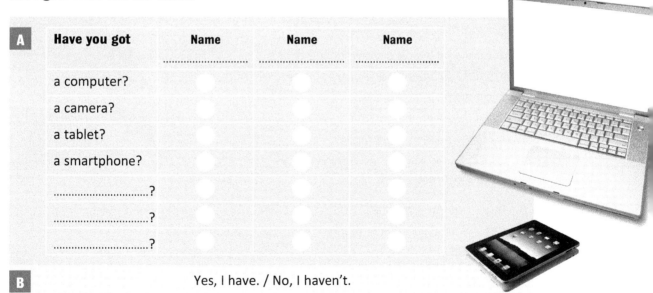

A Have you got	Name	Name	Name
a computer?			
a camera?			
a tablet?			
a smartphone?			
...................?			
...................?			
...................?			

B   Yes, I have. / No, I haven't.

8 **Work in pairs. Ask and answer about other things you have got like pets, a mountain bike etc.**

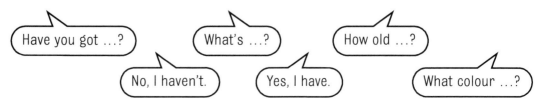

Have you got ...?   What's ...?   How old ...?

No, I haven't.   Yes, I have.   What colour ...?

Grammar

have got

1 Look at the dialogue on page 44 and complete the table below.

Positive			
I / you / we / they	**have / 've**	got	dark hair.
He / she / it	[1]............ **/ 's**		blue eyes.

Negative			
I / you / we / they	**have not /** [3]............	got	a camera.
He / she / it	**has not / hasn't**		big feet.

Questions		
Have I / you / we / they	got	long hair?
[2]............ he / she / it		a football shirt?

Short answers	
Positive	**Negative**
Yes, I / you / we / they **have**.	No, I / you / we / they **haven't**.
Yes, he / she / it [4]................ .	No, he / she / it **hasn't**.

2 Complete the sentences with the positive short form of *have got*.

1 My mum .... a new car.
2 They .... a big house.
3 I .... a nice little dog.
4 My grandma .... a very small garden.
5 She .... a new digital camera.
6 We .... a garage.

3 Look at the picture of the pirate. Circle the correct verb.

1 *He's got / He hasn't got* a beard.
2 *He's got / He hasn't got* a wooden leg.
3 *He's got / He hasn't got* a parrot on his right shoulder.
4 *He's got / He hasn't got* a hat.
5 *He's got / He hasn't got* blonde hair.
6 *He's got / He hasn't got* a hook.

4 Circle the correct word.

1 *Have / Has* you got a car?
2 *Have / Has* he got blonde hair?
3 *Have / Has* they got a house in London?
4 *Have / Has* she got a butterfly on her left shoulder?
5 *Have / Has* you got a euro for me?
6 *Have / Has* your sister got brown eyes?

5 Match the questions and answers.

1 Have you got a computer, Maria?
2 Has your sister got a camera?
3 Has your dad got a car?
4 Have your brothers got mobile phones?
5 Has your dog got brown eyes?
6 Has your computer got a DVD drive?
7 Have you got two tablets, Lisa and Hannah?

a Yes, he has.
b Yes, we have.
c Yes, it has.
d Yes, they have.
e Yes, I have.
f Yes, he has.
g Yes, she has.

Grammar

The article *a / an*

6 **Look at the dialogue on page 44 and complete the table.**

football shirt	**a**pple
photo	**e**ye
¹............ camera	²............ **i**ce cream
pen	**o**ld one
room	**u**mbrella

7 **Look at the table above and complete the rule.**

1 Before a noun that starts with a consonant use ....
2 Before a noun that starts with a vowel use ....

8 **Reorder the words and write sentences and questions.**

1 cat / I've / a / got / .
   I've got a cat.
2 dog / is / There / the / in / garden / a / .
   ....
3 father / teacher / My / is / a / .
   ....

4 house / in / live / a / We / small / .
   ....
5 apple / he / Has / got / an / ?
   ....
6 a / you / Have / bike / got / ?
   ....

9 **Circle the correct word.**

1 He's got *a / an* red car.
2 I've got *an / a* banana.
3 Let's have *a / an* party!

4 Gloria's got *a / an* blue T-shirt.
5 It's *a / an* umbrella.
6 That's *a / an* egg!

10 **Circle the correct word or phrase.**

1 **A** *Have / Has* you got a
     green car?
   B Yes, I have.

2 **A** Has she got a smartphone?
   B Yes, she *has / have*.

3 **A** *Has / Have* he got long hair?
   B Yes, he has!

4 **A** He *haven't / hasn't* got blue eyes.
   B No, he hasn't.

5 **A** *Have / Has* I got something on my head?
   B No, you haven't.

6 **A** *Have / Has* that woman got brown eyes?
   B Yes, she has.

11 **Complete the dialogue.**

Boy ¹.................... you .... ².................... smartphone?
Girl Yes, I ³.................... .
Boy ⁴.................... it good?
Girl Yes, ⁵.................... very good. I ⁶.................... got about 200 apps for it now!
Boy Wow!

 Now do CYBER HOMEWORK 4a www.cambridge.org/elt/more

Skills

Reading

1 **Read the text and complete the profiles on the right.**

I've got four new friends on my
Social networks page! They're
all from the summer course in
Cambridge. Their names are
Gunilla, Mark, Riccardo and
Flavia. Gunilla's got short blonde
hair and blue eyes. She's from
Sweden and she's 15. Flavia's got
long black hair and brown eyes
and she's from Brazil. Riccardo's
got short black hair and glasses.
He's 16 and from Italy. Mark is
British. He's got curly brown hair
and green eyes. He's got a very nice
accent! He's an English teacher!

Name: [1].................... Joreksonn
Nationality: [2]....................
Hair: short, [3]....................
Eye colour: blue
Age: [4]....................

Name: [1].................... Braga
Nationality: [2]....................
Hair: long, [3]....................
Eye colour: [4]....................
Age: 15

Name: [1].................... Rossi
Nationality: [2]....................
Hair: [3]...................., black
Eye colour: brown, wears [4]....................
Age: [5]....................

Name: [1].................... Thompson
Nationality: [2]....................
Hair: [3]...................., brown
Eye colour: [4]....................
Age: 34

Listening

44
CD1

2 **Listen to these interviews and complete the table below.**

	Lizzy Reed	Tom Brooks
Name:	Lizzy Reed	Tom Brooks
Age:	....	....
Colour of eyes:	....	....
Colour of hair:	....	....
Tick the boxes:	tall ☐ short ☐ slim ☐ plump ☐	tall ☐ short ☐ slim ☐ plump ☐
Brothers or sisters?	....	....
Pet?	....	....
Favourite colour?	....	....
Favourite singer?	Robbie Williams	Bruno Mars

Skills

Speaking

3 Work in pairs and describe a famous person to your partner. Your partner can ask you three more questions about him or her and then they guess the name!

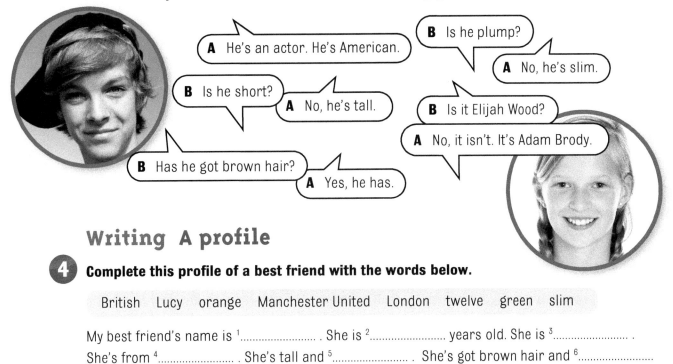

A He's an actor. He's American.

B Is he short?

A No, he's tall.

B Has he got brown hair?

A Yes, he has.

B Is he plump?

A No, he's slim.

B Is it Elijah Wood?

A No, it isn't. It's Adam Brody.

Writing A profile

4 Complete this profile of a best friend with the words below.

> British   Lucy   orange   Manchester United   London   twelve   green   slim

My best friend's name is ¹........................ . She is ²........................ years old. She is ³........................ .
She's from ⁴........................ . She's tall and ⁵........................ . She's got brown hair and ⁶........................
eyes. Her favourite colour is ⁷........................ . Her favourite football team is ⁸........................ .

Tip Names of people, places, football teams and nationalities have capital letters.

5 Now write your own profile for a best friend.

DVD **The Story of the Stones 2** **Don't worry - it's me!**

Watch Episode 1 and match the pictures and the phrases.

1 Try it!   **2** Let go!   **3** What's going on?

CLIL Geography

Continents and nationalities

1 Read the key facts and match the continents and the letters from on the map below.

Key facts!

There are six continents in the world: America, Africa, Australasia, Asia, Europe and Antarctica.

There are two 'poles'. The South Pole is in Antarctica.

The North Pole is not in any continent. It is just ice on the Arctic Ocean.

America ☐ Africa ☐ Australasia ☐ Asia ☐ Europe ☐ Antarctica ☐

2 a There are many countries in each continent. In which continent do you think these countries are? Discuss your answers with a partner.

> I think Japan is in …
> I agree. / No, I think it's in …

| Japan | Morocco | Germany | Nigeria | Spain |
| New Zealand | Brazil | Canada | India | Argentina |

b Now check your answers on a map.

c Look at the nationality words below and complete the sentences. Then check with a partner.

Spanish	1 People from Japan are ....Japanese........ .
German	2 People from New Zealand are ....
Canadian	3 People from Morocco are ....
Brazilian	4 People from Brazil are ....
Indian	5 People from Germany are ....
Moroccan	6 People from Canada are ....
New Zealanders	7 People from India are ....
Japanese	8 People from Spain are ....

3 Now circle the continent and country you are from on the map and complete the sentence.

I'm from .... I'm .... is in ....

WEBQUEST
- Pick a continent and find out about two countries in it.
- Talk about the geography of the countries and what the people look like.

 Go to www.cambridge.org/elt/more for extra CLIL

Check your progress 2

1 **Write the opposites. [½ point each]**

1 big - ....
2 early - ....
3 unfriendly - ....
4 bad - ....
5 old - ....
6 happy - ....

☐ **3**

2 **Write the nationalities.**

1 Britain ....
2 France ....
3 China ....
4 Italy ....
5 Switzerland ....
6 The USA ....

☐ **6**

3 **Complete the sentences with *There is / There are / There isn't / There aren't*.**

1 .... a desk in my bedroom. ☑
2 .... many posters in my room. ☒
3 .... a green rug. ☒
4 .... blue curtains. ☑
5 .... a big bookcase. ☑

☐ **5**

4 **Reorder the words.**

1 two / I've / brothers / got / .
....
2 hasn't / garden / a / got / She / .
....
3 he / new / got / Has / car / a / ?
....
4 got / They / computer / have / a / .
....
5 Have / eyes / got / green / you / ?
....

☐ **5**

5 **Complete the questions and answers. [2 points each]**

1 .... Tom .... a mobile phone?
.... ☑
2 .... they .... an umbrella?
.... ☒
3 .... you .... brown hair?
.... ☑

4 .... Sally .... glasses?
.... ☑
5 .... you .... the English books?
.... ☑
6 .... it .... a garage?
.... ☒

☐ **12**

6 **Write the sentences using the negative form.**

1 She has got a big dog.
....
2 They have got a mobile phone.
....
3 I have got black hair.
....
4 You have got a sister.
....
5 We have got a new DVD.
....
6 Dad has got blue eyes.
....

☐ **6**

7 **Complete the dialogue.**

A [1]................... car is this?
B It isn't Jack's. Jack [2]................... a car.
A [3]................... you .... a car, Melissa?
B Yes, I [4]................... and I [5]................... a bicycle, too.
A [6]................... bicycles are they?
B [7]................... Ben and Jenny's.

☐ **7**

8 **Translate the sentences.**

1 There is a big dog in the garden.
....
2 Is there a computer on the desk?
....
3 There aren't any bags on the floor.
....
4 Have you got a red umbrella?
....
5 John hasn't got any brothers or sisters.
....
6 What colour hair have you got?
....

☐ **6**

TOTAL ☐ **50**

MY PROGRESS SO FAR IS... brilliant! ☐ quite good. ☐ not great. ☐

UNIT 5 I never eat chips!

45
CD1
1 Listen and read.

Waitress	Hello. What would you like to eat?
Adam	Um, can I have a cheeseburger, please?
Waitress	Would you like chips with that?
Adam	Yes, please! And a coke, thanks.
Waitress	OK. And for you? Would you like a burger too?
Leah	No, thanks. Can I have an egg salad, please, and some water?
Adam	What about chips?
Leah	I never eat chips!
Adam	Well, I never eat salad.
Leah	But it's good for you! I try and eat healthy food every day, Adam.
Adam	Really? I try and eat chips every day!
Leah	They're aren't very good for you, Adam!
Waitress	Here you are!

(later)

Leah	Mmm, this salad is delicious. And it's so healthy!
Adam	Mmm, this *burger* is delicious. And the chips are great, too … Hey, those are my chips! You never eat chips, remember?
Leah	Sorry, Adam. But they're delicious. Have some salad!
Adam	OK. Mm. It's very good.

You learn
- present simple
- spelling 3rd person singular
- adverbs of frequency
- words for food / in a restaurant

and then you can
- make and reply to offers and requests
- talk about favourite food

Dialogue work

2 Circle T (True) or F (False) for the sentences below.

1 Leah doesn't want a cheeseburger. **T / F**
2 Leah wants a coke. **T / F**
3 Leah has salad once a week. **T / F**
4 Adam wants chips. **T / F**
5 Adam likes Leah's salad. **T / F**
6 Leah hates Adam's chips. **T / F**

3 **a Read the dialogue on page 54 again and complete the dialogue below.**

Waitress   What would you like to eat?
Adam   Can I have a ¹..., please?
Waitress   Would you like ²... with that?
Adam   Yes, please! And a coke, thanks.

b Act out other dialogues using different foods.

Replying to offers

4 **Listen and circle the words you hear.**

1 **A** banana / apple
  B Yes, please. / No, thanks.

2 **A** orange / apple
  B Yes, please. / No, thanks.

3 **A** sandwich / hamburger
  B Yes, please. / No, thanks.

4 **A** ice cream / yoghurt
  B Yes, please. / No, thanks.

Talking about favourite foods

5 **Listen and tick the food you hear, then talk about Kate and Mark.**

Kate likes:	
☐ apples	☐ salad
☐ oranges	☐ spinach
☐ bananas	☐ carrots
☐ kiwis	☐ potatoes

Kate likes …

She eats …

Mark likes:	
☐ hamburgers	☐ fish
☐ rice	☐ chicken
☐ pizza	☐ oranges
☐ noodles	☐ grapes

Mark likes …

He always eats …

Vocabulary

Food

  1 **Listen and repeat.**

onions

tea

eggs

rice

bread

fish

cherries

chicken

oranges

milk

potatoes

coffee

sausages

grapes

spinach

apples

carrots

orange juice

2 Write the words from exercise 1 in the correct category.

Drinks	Vegetables	Fruit	Meat	Others

In a restaurant

  3 **Write the numbers next to the correct word, then listen and check.**

bottle ☐

fork ☐

spoon ☐

knife ☐

plate ☐

napkin ☐

tablecloth ☐

glass ☐

cup and saucer ☐

Communication

Sounds right /ɪ/ and /iː/

50 CD1

4

a Listen and repeat.

1 h**e** sh**e** m**ee**t cr**ea**m fourt**ee**n

2 **i**t h**i**s f**i**sh s**i**x ch**i**cken

51 CD1

b Listen and repeat.

1 His name's Steve. He's fourteen.

2 Meet his dog – she's six!

Talking about what you eat

5

a Complete the questionnaire.

How healthy are you?

How often do you eat:	often	sometimes	never
apples?	☐	☐	☐
chocolate?	☐	☐	☐
pizza?	☐	☐	☐
spinach?	☐	☐	☐
fish?	☐	☐	☐
oranges?	☐	☐	☐
chicken?	☐	☐	☐
sausages?	☐	☐	☐
How often do you drink:			
tea / coffee?	☐	☐	☐
herbal tea?	☐	☐	☐
water?	☐	☐	☐
fruit juice?	☐	☐	☐

Good!

Not so good!

Foods that are good for you:	Foods that are not so good for you:
apples, spinach, fish, oranges, chicken	chocolate, pizza, sausages
Drinks that are good for you:	**Drinks that are not so good for you:**
water, herbal tea	coffee, tea, fruit juice (often contains a lot of sugar)

b Discuss your answers with a partner.

A I often eat *apples*. What about you?

B *Sometimes. / No, never. / Yes, always.*

6 **Write and say what you eat for:**

breakfast. ....

lunch. ....

dinner. ....

What's your favourite food? ....

Grammar

Present simple Positive

1 **Read the examples and complete the table.**

| I eat salad every week. | My dad loves it. | She eats it every day. |

| I / you / we / they | love | salad. |
| He / she / it | 1 .... | |

2 **Circle the correct word.**

1 I *wash* / *washes* my bike on Fridays.
2 She *loves* / *love* curry and rice.
3 We *hate* / *hates* football.
4 You *teach* / *teaches* Italian at our school.

5 He *studies* / *study* French with me.
6 They *watch* / *watches* TV at the weekends.
7 We *go* / *goes* to the cinema on Sundays.
8 She *takes* / *take* the bus to school.

Spelling 3rd person singular

Notice the spelling.

Rela**x**	My dad always relax**es** after Sunday breakfast.
Ki**ss**	She kiss**es** her mum goodbye every morning.
Wa**sh**	He wash**es** his bike on Saturdays.
D**o**	Mary do**es** the shopping.
Carr**y**	Steve carr**ies** the shopping for his mum.
Wat**ch**	Jenny watch**es** DVDs every day.

3 **Complete the third person singular form of these verbs. Use the Present simple.**

1 I eat   he ....*eats*.......
2 I work   she ....
3 I tidy   she ....
4 I go   it ....

5 I like   he ....
6 I mix   he ....
7 I cry   she ....
8 I do   she ....

9 I pass   he ....
10 I study   he ....
11 I play   it ....
12 I watch   she ....

4 **Reorder the words and write sentences in the Present simple.**

1 Paul / on / Saturday / mornings / visits / grandparents / his / .
   Paul visits his grandparents on Saturday mornings. ....

2 parents / My / in / France / spend / their holidays / .
   ....

3 brother / goes / to work / His / eight o'clock / at / .
   ....

4 wears / that / T-shirt / every day / She / to / school / .
   ....

5 play / on / football / They / in the park / friends / with / their / Sundays / .
   ....

Grammar

Adverbs of frequency

5 **Read the examples and complete the rule.**

I **often** play football.   I am **never** late.

Frequency adverbs usually go [1]......................... the main verb.
But they go [2]......................... the verb *be*.

100%	I always	
	I usually	
	I often	eat popcorn at the cinema.
	I sometimes	
0%	I never	

6 **Write the words in the correct place on the scale.**

sometimes   never   always   often   usually

0% ————————————————————————————————→ 100%

1......................... 2......................... 3......................... 4......................... 5.........................

7 **Reorder the words and write sentences.**

1 beef / eat / never / I

....

2 She's / hungry / always

....

3 take / an / I / to school / always / apple

....

4 for school / late / usually / He's

....

5 go / to a restaurant / They / sometimes

....

6 She / on Sundays / often / goes / to the cinema

....

7 do / I / on Saturdays / homework / never

....

8 are / We / at school / on Mondays / usually

....

8 **Write the sentences correctly using the words in brackets.**

1 We .... to a restaurant. (go sometimes)

2 He .... fish. (eats never)

3 I .... on Sunday. (curry eat usually)

4 I'm .... in the morning. (hungry never)

5 She .... bananas. (eats always)

Now do **CYBER HOMEWORK** 5a www.cambridge.org/elt/more

Reading

1 Read the texts and write: *unhealthy*, *healthy* or *very healthy* under them.

Healthy Eating!

Max I usually have a burger and chips for lunch! I sometimes have chicken and chips. I never eat vegetables. I hate them. My sister likes spinach but I hate it. I often drink coke. It's bad for you, I know. I don't like water. It's boring!

....

Richard My mum always cooks dinner. My favourite dish is fish pie. That's fish with potatoes. We usually have it twice a week. We always have vegetables with it. My favourite vegetable is spinach. I also like fruit. I love cherries. I usually drink water.

....

Katy For lunch, I usually have vegetable soup or I sometimes have chicken with salad. I don't like chips and I don't like red meat. Oh, and I always eat fruit. I love oranges. I usually drink water. I hate fizzy drinks, especially coke.

....

Olga My mum usually makes soup for dinner. Then we often have meat or chicken with vegetables and potatoes. My favourite vegetable is beans. I don't like spinach or broccoli. For pudding, we often have ice cream. We sometimes have cake. My favourite is chocolate cake. My sister's favourite is carrot cake. My mum makes really good cakes!

....

Eva I usually have warm milk for breakfast and I always have an egg with some toast. I never have butter on my toast. Then I have some fruit. I sometimes have a banana but I usually have an apple.

....

2 Now circle the correct words.

1 Eva *always* / *never* has an egg for breakfast.
2 Katy *loves* / *hates* coke.
3 Max *often* / *never* eats vegetables for lunch.
4 Olga *often* / *sometimes* has ice cream for dessert.
5 Richard has fish *twice a week* / *every day*.

Skills

3 Circle T (True) or F (False).

1 Max never eats vegetables.	**T / F**
2 Katy sometimes has salad at lunch.	**T / F**
3 Eva never has fruit for breakfast.	**T / F**
4 Olga often eats spinach.	**T / F**
5 Richard never drinks water with his meals.	**T / F**

Listening and speaking

4 Listen to the students below, then listen again and complete the table with the correct adverb of frequency.

always
usually
often
sometimes
never

	Sarah	Ben	Chris
chicken			
meat			
burger			
chips			
salad			
vegetables			
fruit			
ice cream			
rice			
fish			
cake			

5 Now ask a friend about what they eat.

> **A** What do you usually have for breakfast, lunch, dinner?

> **B** I usually have …

Writing A short text

6 Complete the paragraph for yourself. Use adverbs of frequency.

> **The Food I Eat**
>
> I .... fish. I .... chicken. I .... vegetables.
> I .... fruit. I .... biscuits and cakes.
> For breakfast, I usually have ....
> For lunch, I usually have ....
> For dinner, I usually have ....

Culture

School in England

In Britain, children go to school between the ages of 5 and 16. This is called compulsory education and it is free. Schools teach the National Curriculum, which is divided into Key Stages. Students do tests at the end of each Key Stage.

Most students eat their lunch in the school canteen. Some students bring their own lunch, others buy a meal in the canteen.

Most schools encourage sports and have their own teams. Popular sports are football, hockey, basketball and athletics.

Students don't usually wear a uniform at Sixth Form College.

The facts

Primary School

Children go to primary school between the ages of 5 and 11.

Age 5–7   Key Stage 1
Age 7–11   Key Stage 2

At the end of Key Stage 2, students choose a secondary school.

Secondary School

Age 11–14   Key Stage 3
Age 14–16   Key Stage 4

At the end of Key Stage 4, students do GCSE (General Certificate of Secondary Education) exams.

When they are 16, students can choose to leave school or to stay at school for another two years and study for their A-levels. You usually need three A-levels in order to go to university. You can study for A-levels at secondary school or at Sixth Form College.

Public schools

In Britain, 'public schools' are private and students have to pay fees in order to study there. There are more than 250 public schools and they are usually very expensive. The fees can cost up to £10,000 a term.

Work in pairs and answer the questions.

1 What age do children start school in your country?
2 What types of schools are there?
3 When does compulsory education stop?
4 What tests must students do?

More! Online Action Box Listening and Quiz online.

Write a text for the MORE! Online journal. Put it online for students from other countries to read.

➤ Go to www.cambridge.org/elt/more for extra CULTURE

Extra Reading

INTERNATIONAL **CRIME BUSTERS** EUROPE

The International Crime Busters are flying into Athens.

A ship at the bottom of the sea. Missing submarines. Treasure! Are you excited?

Yes, I am, Nick!

1

The ship is under the sea, here. We know there is treasure on it, but every time we send down a minisub, it never comes back. Someone doesn't want us to find the treasure!

Someone or something? Let's find out.

2

This is the only way to solve the mystery.

Yes, let's go underwater.

3

Look! There's the ship.

Yes, but there's no one and nothing there!

4

What's that?!

I'm not sure. But I think it is our mystery.

5

Look, I think he wants to eat our minisub! Fire a rocket at him!

Yes! Take that!

6

He's quick!

Yes, he is! He just catches them!

7

Fire another one! I think he's scared now!

8

Look, he can't move now. Let's get him!

9

There are no monsters now! It's safe to look for the treasure.

And there is lots of it!

Thank you, Crime Busters.

10

UNIT 6 I go to bed at ten

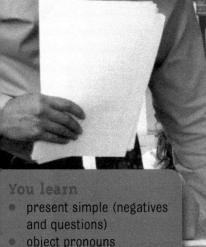

You learn
- present simple (negatives and questions)
- object pronouns
- words for daily activities

and then you can
- ask and tell the time
- talk about routines

54
CD1

1 **Listen and read.**

Mr Jones	Who's got the answer to question 5? Joe?
	(Joe snores)
Mr Jones	Joe! Wake up! You're in the classroom! You aren't at home in bed!
Joe	Sorry, Mr Jones. I'm tired!
Mr Jones	What's the matter? Are you ill?
Joe	No, I'm not. But my life is very hard.
Mr Jones	Oh dear. Why? What do you do every day?
Joe	Well, I get up early every morning. I wake up at seven o'clock, and have breakfast. Then I go to school. I work hard at school every day, and after lunch, I do sports. Then I go home and do my homework. I help my mum in the house, and tidy my room. Then I have dinner and finish my homework. I go to bed at ten o'clock.
Mr Jones	But why do you go to bed so late? Do you have a lot of homework to do?
Joe	No, I don't have a lot of homework, Mr Jones.
Mr Jones	What do you do every night, then, until ten?
Joe	I watch TV and play computer games for three hours.
Mr Jones	That sounds like a very hard life!

Dialogue work

2 **Read the dialogue again and circle the correct answer.**

1 Joe is *tired / sad*.
2 He *wakes up / gets up* at seven o'clock.
3 He *goes to bed / watches TV* at ten o'clock.
4 He *does / doesn't* have a lot of homework to do.
5 He *does / doesn't* have time to watch TV and play computer games.

3 **Work in pairs. Invent dialogues.**

A What's the matter with you?

B I'm *bored / tired / hungry*.

Asking and telling the time

55
CD1

4 **Listen and repeat the times.**

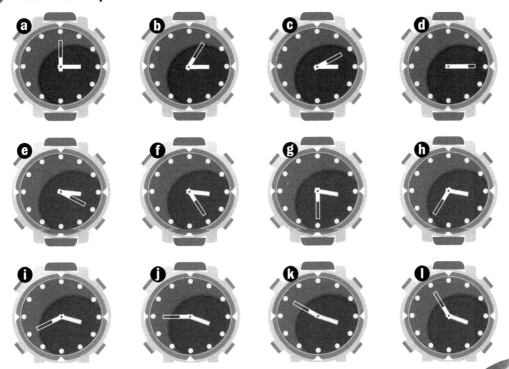

5 **Work in pairs. Point to a clock and ask and answer about the times.**

A What's the time?

B It's half past three.

6 **Say what you usually do at the times below.**

| 8.30 am | 1 pm | 4 pm | 6 pm |
| 7 pm | 9-10 pm |

Tip Note!

am = in the morning (before 12 am)
pm = in the afternoon (after 12 am)

I usually get to school at 8.30 am.

Vocabulary

Daily activities

1 Listen and write the number of the correct picture next to the verb.

watch TV `1`

read a book ☐

take the dog for a walk ☐

play the piano ☐

hang out with friends ☐

surf the web ☐

do homework ☐

listen to music ☐

play football ☐

go rollerblading ☐

play computer games ☐

go shopping ☐

Sounds right! Days of the week (revision)

2 Listen and repeat.

Monday, Tuesday, Wednesday – sad!
Thursday, Friday – they aren't bad!
Saturday and Sunday – great!
Tomorrow's Monday – don't be late!

3 Work in pairs. Ask and answer.

A Today's Friday. What day is tomorrow?

B Saturday.

B Yes.

B Today's Tuesday. What day is tomorrow?

Communication

Talking about routines

 4 **a** **Complete the questionnaire, then ask three other students.**

> **A** Do you surf the web every day?

> **B** Yes, I do. / No, I don't.

Do you:	Me:	Name:	Name:	Name:
surf the web every day?				
go shopping with your mum on Saturdays?				
play any sports at the weekend?				
play an instrument?				
play computer games every day?				
listen to music every day?				
watch television every evening?				
read a lot?				

b **Talk about your answers with the class.**

> Marco surfs the web every day, but he doesn't play any sports at the weekend.

Talking about time

 5 **Circle the correct words, then listen and check. Practise the dialogues in pairs.**

1 **A** What's the *time / clock*?
   B It's twenty-five to eight.

2 **A** It's half *past / to* three in the afternoon.
   B Oh, no! I'm late!

3 **A** What time is it *in / for* London?
   B It's 7 pm.

4 **A** Excuse me, what time is it?
   B It's quarter *to / at* eleven.

5 **A** Is it *early / midday* now?
   B Yes, it is. It's two minutes past twelve.

6 **A** What time is it, please?
   B I don't know. I can't see the *clock / half an hour*.

Grammar

Present simple Negative

1 **Look at the dialogue on page 64 and complete the table.**

Present simple negative

I / you / we / they	[1].................... have a lot of homework.
He / she / it	doesn't live here.

2 **Circle the correct word.**

1 They *don't / doesn't* like fish soup.
2 I *don't / doesn't* eat a lot of chocolate.
3 Emily *don't / doesn't* know how to cook an egg!
4 Harry and Ron don't *play / plays* computer games.
5 Dad doesn't *know / knows* how to drive.

3 **Circle the correct negative form.**

I always go rollerblading in the park at weekends. My best friend, Tina, [1]*don't / doesn't* like rollerblading. She plays football but I [2]*don't / doesn't* like that! My brothers [3]*doesn't / don't* do a lot of sport. They watch it on TV but they [4]*don't / doesn't* play or do anything! I [5]*don't / doesn't* want to spend all my time in front of the TV so I go out! My mum [6]*don't / doesn't* watch TV either – she reads, all the time!

4 **Complete the text with the words below.**

> cooks   live   makes   works
> buys   doesn't (x2)

Hi, I'm Eamon from Dublin in Ireland.
I [1]............................ with my three brothers and two sisters. My mum [2]........................... work. She's always at home. My dad [3]...........................
three days a week. When he's at home, he
[4]........................... . We like that because the food he [5]........................... is lovely! My mother
[6]........................... cook. She [7]...........................
a lot of meals from the supermarket!

Present simple Questions and short answers

5 **Look at the dialogue on page 64 and complete the table.**

Questions

[1]....................	I / you / we / they	have a lot of homework to do?
Does	he / she / it	go to bed at 9 o'clock?

Short answers

Positive	Yes, I / you / we / they **do**.
	Yes, he / she / it **does**.
Negative	No, I / you / we / they **don't**.
	No, he / she / it **doesn't**.

6 **Circle the correct word.**

1 *Do / Does* you play an instrument?
2 *Does / Do* Shane like computer games?
3 *Do / Does* your brother go rollerblading?
4 *Does / Do* your sister play football?
5 *Do / Does* you like your new trainers?
6 *Does / Do* they go shopping at weekends?

7 **Write answers for the questions in exercise 6.**

1 Yes, ...
2 No, ...
3 Yes, ...
4 Yes, ...
5 Yes, ...
6 No, ...

Grammar

8 **Write questions and answers.**

1 you / know / how to speak German (✗)
.... ?
....

2 Adriano / speak / English (✓)
.... ?
....

3 the boys / go / to the sports centre / at the weekend (✓)
....
.... ?
....

4 your teacher / explain / everything (✗)
.... ?
....

5 your parents / like / computer games (✗)
.... ?
....

6 the lesson / finish / at 4 pm (✓)
.... ?
....

9 **Complete the sentences with *Do* or *Does*.**

1 .... you go to bed early every night?
2 .... your mother work?
3 .... you get to school at 8.30 am?
4 .... your family have a car?
5 .... you have a lot of homework to do every night?

10 **Now answer the questions above.**

....
....
....
....
....
....
....
....
....
....
....

Object pronouns

11 **Complete the table with the words below.**

him	them	us	me
her	you	it	you

Subject pronouns		Object pronouns
I	→	1 ....
you	→	2 ....
he	→	3 ....
she	→	4 ....
it	→	5 ....
we	→	6 ....
you	→	6 ....
they	→	8 ....

12 **Circle the correct object pronoun.**

1 This is Harry. Do you know *him* / *her*?
2 Look at these new photos!! We love *them* / *her*.
3 I don't know how to do this exercise. Can you help *her* / *me*, please?
4 The dog's hungry! Feed *it* / *them*, please.
5 We're tired now. Can you take *us* / *we* home, please?

13 **Complete the sentences with the correct object pronouns.**

1 This is Mike. He's my brother-in-law. My sister is married to ....
2 **A** Where is Sue?
   B Paul is at home with .... She isn't well.
3 Mark and Sarah! Take these jackets with ....
4 **A** Do you know .... ?
   B Yes, that's Leo.
5 The Smiths aren't here. We are going without .... !
6 At Christmas, my aunt takes .... all to the theatre; Mum, Dad, my brothers and me.
7 I haven't got any money with .... I can't pay!

Now do CYBER HOMEWORK 6a www.cambridge.org/elt/more

Skills

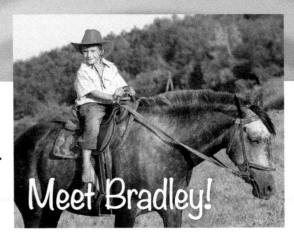

Meet Bradley!

Reading

1 Read the text and circle T (True) or F (False). Correct the sentences that are false.

Hi! I'm Bradley. I live with my mother and father and two sisters on a sheep farm in northern Australia. We don't live near other people so I spend a lot of time on my own, but it's fun. There is a river near my house and I've got a horse so I can ride when I want. It's cool living here. The big city is one and a half hours away by bus.

I get up at half past six, then have breakfast. At seven, I leave the house and walk for ten minutes to the school bus stop.

School starts at nine and ends at four. I get home at half past five. Then I help my father, ride my horse or play ball with my sisters.

Dinner is at seven. After that, I do my homework, play computer games or watch TV with Mum and Dad.

On Saturdays or Sundays I go to the river to fish. I often catch barramundi. Sometimes, we have barramundi for dinner!

1 Bradley lives in the north of America.	**T / F**
2 He gets up at half past six.	**T / F**
3 His dad takes him to school.	**T / F**
4 School starts at nine o'clock.	**T / F**
5 He comes home at six pm three days a week.	**T / F**
6 He rides his horse after school.	**T / F**
7 Dinner is at eight o'clock.	**T / F**
8 At weekends, Bradley goes fishing.	**T / F**

Listening

59
CD1

2 Listen and circle the correct word(s).

1 Kate gets up at quarter past *seven / six*.

2 She takes the dog for a walk at *half / quarter* past six.

3 Kate practises the piano for *one hour / two hours* in the morning.

4 They eat breakfast at *half / twenty* past seven.

5 Kate finishes school at half past *five / three*.

6 Kate practises the piano for *one hour / two hours* in the evening.

Skills

Speaking

60 CD1

3 **Listen and repeat, then interview your partner.**

A Can I interview you for a school project?

B Yes, go ahead.

A OK, first question. When do you get up in the morning?

B *At quarter to seven.*

A And when do you leave for school?

B *At quarter past eight.*

A And when do you do your homework?

B *Usually from five to six.*

A Thanks!

Writing Connecting words

Tip Remember!
We use words like **'and'** and **'then'** to make connections in a text.

4 **Read the text and circle the connecting words.**

MY DAY!

I get up at half past five and I have breakfast at quarter past six. My dad goes to work at half past six and he takes me to school in his car. Then I wait in the cafeteria for school to start. Our school starts at eight o'clock and it ends at half past one. In the afternoon, I do my homework, then I hang out with my friends, read or play computer games. I watch TV from five to six. We have dinner at seven. At nine o'clock, I go to bed.

5 **Write a text similar to the one above about your day.**

DVD The Story of the Stones 3 Don't be scared!

Complete the dialogue. Watch Episode 3 again to check.

Go on
But it's true
Well done
Promise

Daniel	Don't make fun of me!
Sarah	...............................!
Emma	.... Daniel. Rub your stone!
Daniel	No, I don't want to.
Sarah	OK. Me first, then you. Promise?
Daniel	...............................!
Sarah	Great, Daniel! ....!

CLIL Science

A Healthy Diet

1 Read the key facts. What are the four main food groups we need to stay healthy?

Key facts!

Our bodies need a balanced diet to work well. The four main food groups are carbohydrates, proteins, fats and fibres. There are vitamins and minerals in these foods. Each of them does a specific job for our bodies.

To stay healthy, drink enough water and eat the correct amount of food from the four groups.

2 a Look at the food pyramid below. This shows the correct amount of each food group we need for a healthy diet.

b Complete the sentences with the name of the correct food group.

1 ...., ... and .... like tomatoes, beans and bananas help us digest our food.

2 .... like bread, cereal and potatoes give us fuel and energy.

3 .... like meat, milk and nuts helps us grow and repair our body.

4 .... like butter, oil, cakes, sweets etc and cheese give us energy.

1 Fats and sugars

2 Protein

3 Fibre, Fruit and Vegetables

4 Carbohydrates

3 Draw the foods you eat for breakfast, lunch and dinner. Now compare them with a partner. Whose diet is healthier?

I usually have toast, tea and an egg for breakfast. What about you?

I have ...

WEBQUEST

Find out:
- What is genetically modified food? Do you think it is a good idea?
- What is a Mediterranean diet? How healthy is it?

Go to www.cambridge.org/elt/more for extra **CLIL**

Check your progress 3

1 **Reorder the letters to write food words.**
[½ point each]

1 kncehci ....
2 egsusaa ....
3 edarb ....
4 ihsnpca ....
5 topatpo ....
6 innoo ....

☐ **3**

2 **Complete the daily activities.**

1 .... a book.
2 .... computer games.
3 .... with friends.
4 .... music.
5 .... the web.
6 .... the dog for a walk.

☐ **6**

3 **Reorder the words and write sentences.**

1 walk / park / They / to / usually / the / .
   ....
2 late / never / school / She / for / is / .
   ....
3 cinema / go / sometimes / Saturday / We / the / on / to / .
   ....
4 Mark / day / vegetables / eats / every / .
   ....
5 dinner / for / pasta / often / eat / We / .
   ....

☐ **5**

4 **Circle the correct word.**

1 We *doesn't* / *don't* play football every day.
2 *Does* / *Do* Sally go to the cinema every Friday?
3 Harry *does* / *doesn't* have a new car.
4 *Do* / *Does* they study English at school?
5 I *doesn't* / *don't* like rollerblading.

☐ **5**

5 **Complete the questions and answers.**
[2 points each]

1 .... you usually walk to school?
   ....
2 .... your teacher speak English?
   ....
3 .... you eat pizza once a week?
   ....
4 .... your English lesson finish now?
   ....

5 .... your friend like football?
   ....
6 .... you and your friends like computer games?
   ....

☐ **12**

6 **Write the sentences using the negative form.**

1 They like fish.
   ....
2 Paul eats a healthy lunch every day.
   ....
3 I watch TV every evening.
   ....
4 We play volleyball twice a week.
   ....
5 Dad does the shopping on Saturday.
   ....
6 She walks to work.
   ....

☐ **6**

7 **Complete the dialogue.**

A [1].................. you like pizza?
B Yes, [2].................. .
A [3].................. you and Adam like hamburgers?
B [4]No, ...
A [5].................. Dave eat rice?
B Yes, [6].................. but he [7].................. eat pasta.

☐ **7**

8 **Translate the questions and sentences.**

1 Do you tidy your bedroom every week?
   ....
2 Does your sister play computer games?
   ....
3 They don't go to school on Sunday.
   ....
4 He doesn't know her.
   ....
5 Do they live in Dublin?
   ....
6 She doesn't like fish.
   ....

☐ **6**

TOTAL ☐ **50**

MY PROGRESS SO FAR IS... brilliant! ☐ quite good. ☐ not great. ☐

Go to www.cambridge.org/elt/more for **MORE!** training

You learn
- demonstrative adjectives and pronouns
- countable and uncountable nouns
- *How much? / How many?*
- *some / any*
- words for clothes

and then you can
- talk about prices
- talk about clothes

02
CD2

1 **Listen and read.**

Adam	I want to buy a present for my sister. It's her birthday tomorrow.
Kelly	This is a nice picture.
Adam	How much is it?
Kelly	£7.99. How much money have you got?
Adam	£10.00. But I want to buy this T-shirt. Can I try this on, please?
Assistant	Of course.
Kelly	Why do you want to try it on? It's for your sister.
Adam	No, it isn't for her. It's for me!
Kelly	But it's £6.99!.......

(10 minutes later)

	Now you've only got £3.01 left! There aren't any nice clothes for that price, Adam!
Adam	Hold on, these socks are nice. Excuse me, how much are these socks?
Assistant	They're £3.99.
Adam	Oh dear ...
Assistant	But those red ones are £2.99!
Adam	Great! So I've got a new T-shirt, and my sister's got some red socks! Let's go and buy the card now! Erm, can you lend me some money?

Dialogue work

2 Read the dialogue again and correct the wrong information in each sentence.

1 Adam wants to buy a present for his ~~mother~~.   *sister*
2 It's her birthday today.   ....
3 The picture is £6.99.   ....
4 Adam's got £20.00.   ....
5 The T-shirt is for Adam's sister.   ....
6 The red socks are £3.99.   ....

Tip   £ = pound   p = pence $ = dollar   € = euro

Talking about prices

03 CD2 **3** Listen and repeat the prices.

£28 $39   €47   £52   £65 $73   £81   €99   €100

04 CD2 **4** Guess the price of the objects, then listen and check.

£179.00   £34.99   £16.99   £3.50   £5.00   £36.50

£8.99   99p   £9.99   £2.50   £1.99   £69.99

I think the sweets are …

I think the key-ring is …

I think the mobile phone is …

mobile phone

magazine

T-shirt

sweets

MP3 player

key-ring

computer game

dog food

book

CD

DVD

jeans

05 CD2 **5** Listen to the dialogues and act them out, then invent another.

Dialogue 1

Boy   How much are the trainers?
Shop assistant They're £29.99.
Boy   And the T-shirt?
Shop assistant It's £6.99. Or two for £9.99.
Boy   Thank you.

Dialogue 2

Shop assistant Yes, please?
Girl   How much is the DVD? There's no price on it.
Shop assistant They're all £12.99.
Girl   Thank you.

Vocabulary

Clothes

1 Listen and write the missing words, then listen and repeat.

Describing clothes

2 Ask and answer questions about the clothes in the picture above.

A What colour's the dress?
B It's green, pink and white …

A What colour are the jeans?
B They're …

3 a Describe the photos below.

casual

He's got a top with a hood …

hood

SMART

b Now describe your clothes to a partner.

Communication

Talking about clothes

4 Interview your partner.

Questions:	Answers:

Do you buy your own clothes?
Do you get clothes for your birthday?
Do you wear T-shirts with animals?
Do you wear pink clothes?
Do you wear jeans with holes?
Do you wear caps?
Do you wear a ring?
Do you like red / blue / …?

Yes, I do.

No, I don't.

5 Ask and answer questions about someone in your class. A must guess who it is.

A Does he sometimes wear *blue jeans*?
B Yes, he does.
A Does he often wear *brown shoes*?
B No, he doesn't.
A Does he always *wear T-shirts*?
B *Yes, he does*.
A Is it John?
B *Yes, it is / No, it isn't.*

Buying clothes in a shop

07
CD2

6 Listen and circle the correct words to complete the dialogue.

A Excuse me. How ¹*much / lot* are these jeans?
B They're £50.00. ²*Do / Does* you like them?
A Yes, I ³*do / does*! But I haven't got £50.
B I have got jeans for £25.
A ⁴*Where / What* are they?
B Look! ⁵*Those / That* jeans in the window are £25.
A Oh! They're nice! I'd like a black ⁶*pair / one*, please.

7 Write a new dialogue and act it out for the class.

Grammar

Demonstrative adjectives and pronouns

1 Match the sentences and the pictures.

1 I like these trainers.
2 I like those trainers.
3 How much are these DVDs?
4 How much are those DVDs?
5 Don't drink that water!
6 Don't drink this water!

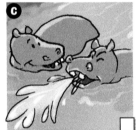

2 Look at the pictures and complete the table.

Do you like
¹.......... top?
².......... top's nice.
³.......... trousers are nice.
How much are
⁴.......... trousers?

Countable and uncountable nouns

3 Look at the examples and circle the correct word to complete the rule.

Countable: **boys, houses, trousers, tops.**
Uncountable: **money, food, ham.**
(NOT: moneys, foods, hams)

We *do* / *do not* add an *–s* to uncountable nouns to make them plural.

Uncountable nouns always use the verb in the singular:

The money **is** in my pocket.

Countable nouns use both singular and plural forms of the verb depending on whether they are singular or plural.

The cap **is** here.

The caps **are** on the floor.

4 Write if these nouns are C (Countable) or U (Uncountable).

1 money ....   5 T-shirt ....
2 book ....   6 shoe ....
3 water ....   7 sock ....
4 pasta ....   8 food ....

5 Complete the sentences with *is* or *are*.

1 The pasta .... ready.
2 The socks .... on the floor.
3 The water .... in the bottle.
4 Those houses .... new!
5 This food .... delicious!
6 Those trainers .... cool!!

€ 45.00

Grammar

How much? / How many?

6 Read the examples and complete the rule with *How much* and *How many*.

How much money have you got?
How many T-shirts have you got?

We use ¹.................................... with countable nouns.
We use ².................................... with uncountable nouns.

7 Complete with *How much is* or *How much are*.

1 **A** .... the DVD?
  B It's £11.80.
2 **A** .... the jeans?
  B They're £43.88.
3 **A** .... the T-shirts?
  B They're £6.
4 **A** .... the CD?
  B It's £14.50.
5 **A** .... the shoes?
  B They're £42.99.
6 **A** .... the sweater?
  B It's £23.00

some / any

8 Look at the examples and complete the rules with *some* or *any*.

I haven't got **any** nice clothes.
Have you got **any** money?
She always gives me **some** money.
I want **some** new trousers.

With uncountable and countable plural nouns:
use ¹.............................. in positive sentences.
use ².............................. in negative sentences.
use ³.............................. in questions.

9 Complete the text with *some* or *any*.

My brother's room is so messy! There are clothes all over the floor. There are ¹........................ shirts near the window and ²........................ T-shirts under the bed. Are there ³........................ trainers? Yes, there are! Three pairs behind the door. There aren't ⁴........................ shoes and there aren't ⁵........................ sweaters. But there are ⁶........................ jeans and trousers on the bed. He needs to tidy up his room before Mum comes home.

10 Complete the dialogue with the words below.

| much   some (x2)   any (x2) |

A Have you got ¹........................ money, Sue?
B Yes, how ²........................ do you want?
A Well, I want to buy ³........................ new jeans, so I think about £30.
B Have you got ⁴........................ change? I've got a £50 note.
A Just a minute. Yes, I've got ⁵........................ notes here – two £20s. Here you are.
B And here you are!
A Thanks!

11 Circle the correct word.

What's in this suitcase? Ah! There are ¹*any / some* books and there's ²*some / any* money – lots of money! But there aren't ³*any / some* clothes and there aren't ⁴*some / any* documents. Are there ⁵*any / some* photos? No, I can't see any. I need to go and talk to someone about this!

Skills

Reading

  Read the text from *The Clever Woman* and circle the correct answer below.

One day Sean Murphy is at the bus stop with a friend. He looks very sad.

"What's wrong?" asks his friend.

"I've got a big problem," says Mr Murphy.

"When I go home I'm tired. I want to sit on the sofa and read my book and relax.

But I never relax. I never read my book. When I come home my mother plays the guitar. My wife plays the piano. My two younger children fight and my two older children argue about the television. And the pots and pans are on the cooker."

Mr Murphy's friend listens to him carefully.

Then he says: "Go and see Linda McCormack! She's a very wise woman. She knows the answer to everything."

Linda McCormack listens carefully.

"Have you got any chickens?" she asks him.

Mr Murphy looks confused.

"Yes," he answers. "I've got two chickens!"

"Then bring the chickens into your house," says the wise woman and smiles.

Sean thanks her. Then he rides back home on his bike. He is much happier now.

As soon as he gets home he goes to the hen house and he brings his two chickens into the house.

---

1. Sean Murphy relaxes at home.

   A Right
   B Wrong
   C Doesn't say

2. There are six people in Sean's family.

   A Right
   B Wrong
   C Doesn't say

3. Sean has four chickens at home.

   A Right
   B Wrong
   C Doesn't say

4. Sean also has four dogs.

   A Right
   B Wrong
   C Doesn't say

5. Sean rides a bike.

   A Right
   B Wrong
   C Doesn't say

6. When he gets home, he brings three chickens back into the house.

   A Right
   B Wrong
   C Doesn't say

Skills

Listening

08 CD2

2 **Listen to the next bit of the story and answer the questions.**

1 How many instruments are there in the house?
2 How many geese does Sean bring into the house?
3 How does Sean get to Linda's house?
4 Which animal does Sean bring into the house at the end?
5 How much noise is there in the house?
6 Who is asleep?

Speaking

09 CD2

3 **Work in groups of three. Read the text. How do you think the story finishes? Listen and check.**

Linda says: 'Put the chickens back in the hen house.'

Writing Describing appearance

Tip Use adjectives. Adjectives make sentences interesting.

4 **Read the text below and circle the adjectives.**

My Unusual Friend

My friend loves clothes. Her favourite T-shirt is small and red with a picture of a balloon on it. She often wears it with a denim jacket and skirt and a black cap. She never wears shoes, just pink spotted trainers. She's got long, blonde hair and big, blue eyes and she sometimes paints her nails blue!

She always looks great!

5 **Invent a friend with unusual clothes. Write your own text.**

My friend ....
His / Her favourite .... is ....
He / She often wears ....
He / She never ....
He's / She's got .... hair and .... eyes
and he / she sometimes ....
He / She always looks ....

Culture

Sports in Great Britain

▲ Diane, 15, Swansea, Wales

I play football with the school team. I love football. We train twice a week, three times if there's a match. We usually train after school. Our coach makes us work hard. We start with warm-up exercises and then we practise dribbling or tackling. At the end, we sometimes play a short match. I'm a striker, which means it's my job to score goals. Defenders will do anything to stop you from scoring.

◄ Phillip, 13, Croydon, England

My favourite sport is cricket. Cricket is a team sport and there are 11 players in each team. The teams take turns batting and bowling.
You need to be strong and fast to be a good bowler. When you bowl, you throw the ball to the person on the other team who is batting. They hit the ball as far as they can, then run between 2 sets of sticks called stumps to score runs. The team that is bowling tries to 'bowl out' the batting team by throwing the ball to the stumps before the player finishes a run. The team with the highest number of runs wins. Easy? No!

◄ Emma, 13, Croydon, England

My favourite sport is golf. I practise for two hours every day and I play matches on Saturdays too. I also go to the gym for an hour every day before school. I've got a handicap of four (most adult players never get their handicap under 10). I take part in tournaments all over the country. I play against adults and teenagers of my own age.

Match the names to the definitions below.

1 striker   a   a number given to a player to show how good he/she is
2 coach   b   a person who trains a team
3 bowler   c   a stick used to hit a ball
4 defender   d   kick the ball past another player without losing control
5 dribble   e   a person who scores goals
6 bat   f   a person who throws the ball to the person batting
7 handicap   g   a person who stops players from scoring

Answer the questions about cricket.

1 How many players are in a cricket team?
2 What are the sticks on the cricket field called?
3 How do you 'bowl someone out'?
4 How do you win a match?

> **MORE!**
> **Online Action Box**
> **Listening and Quiz online. Write a text for the MORE! Online journal. Put it online for students from other countries to read.**

 Go to www.cambridge.org/elt/more for extra CULTURE

INTERNATIONAL CRIME BUSTERS EUROPE

11 CD2

1 **Listen and read.**

You learn

- *can* for ability / permission
- *can* questions and short answers
- *like / love / hate doing*
- words for family members

and then you can

- talk about ability
- talk about things you like doing
- ask for permission
- talk about family

Leah and Adam are in the end-of-year school show.

Adam Are your parents here, Leah?

Leah Yes, there they are. Can you see them? That's my mum, in the front row, and that's my dad next to her. And the girl next to him is my sister. Oh, good, Grandpa is here too! That's a surprise.

Adam Why?

Leah Well, he can't hear very well, and he hates listening to pop music! Is your mum here?

Adam Yes. She's just behind your parents! But my dad isn't here. He's working in another country.

Leah Is that your brother?

Adam Yes. He plays in a band, you know.

Leah Really? What does he play?

Adam He plays the guitar, but he can sing too, and he can dance really well … he can do everything!

Leah He's lucky. I can't dance at all. But I love singing.

Adam I love singing too. But I don't like doing it in front of everyone!

Leah Don't worry. We're the best!

Mr Jones *(whispers to kids)* OK, are you ready to start?
(loudly) Welcome to our show, everyone! Here are Leah and Adam, with a song!

Dialogue work

2 Circle T (True) or F (False) for the sentences below.

1	Leah's parents aren't at the show.	**T / F**
2	Leah's grandpa loves listening to pop music.	**T / F**
3	He can't hear very well.	**T / F**
4	Adam's dad isn't at the concert.	**T / F**
5	Adam's brother can sing well.	**T / F**
6	Adam's brother can't play the guitar.	**T / F**
7	Leah can dance well.	**T / F**
8	Adam doesn't like singing.	**T / F**

Talking about ability

3 Look at the pictures and say what you can and can't do.

I can ride horses, but I can't drive a car.

ride horses

drive a car

take good photos

tell jokes

play an instrument

speak German

Talking about family

4 Work in pairs. Bring photos to the class and present members of your family. Say what they can and can't do.

A That's my *uncle / aunt*.
He / She likes riding horses.

B How old is *he / she*?

A *He / She* 's 32.

B What can *he / she* do?

A *He / she can play the piano*.

Asking for permission

5 Listen and repeat, then work in pairs and invent other dialogues.

A Can I go to the *toilet*, please?

B Yes, of course.

A Can I open the *window*, please?

B No, please don't.

A Can I borrow your *pen*, please?

B Sure, here you are.

A Can I borrow your *computer*, please?

B Sorry, it doesn't work.

Vocabulary

Family members

  Listen and write the names.

Lisa   Fred   William   Juliette   Susan   Anthony   Natasha

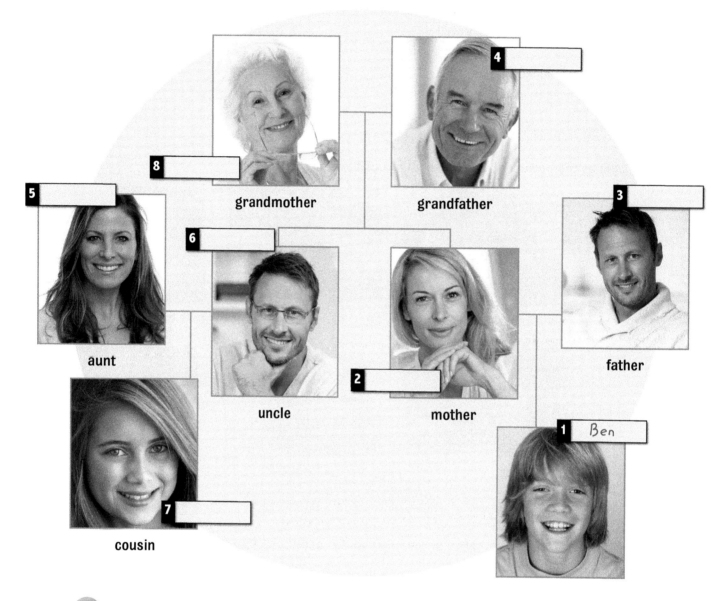

grandmother   grandfather

aunt   uncle   mother   father

cousin

4

8

5

6

3

2

1 Ben

7

2 **Complete the sentences. Use the words below.**

~~son~~
daughter
wife
husband
mother-in-law
father-in-law
brother
sister

1 Ben is Natasha's .... son ....

2 Lisa is William's ....

3 Fred is Natasha's ....

4 Juliette is Susan's ....

5 Natasha is William's ....

6 Anthony is William's ....

7 William is Natasha's ....

8 Natasha is Fred's ....

Communication

Talking about family

3 Work with a partner. Ask and answer questions about the family in exercise 2.

> **A** Is Lisa William's mother-in law?
>
> **B** Yes, that's right.

> **A** Is Juliette Susan's sister?
>
> **B** No, she's her daughter.

4 Work with a partner. Write a list of names of people in your family then ask and answer.

> **A** Who's Suzanne?
>
> **B** She's my aunt.

> **A** Who are Cindy and Jane?
>
> **B** They're my cousins.

Sounds right *Can*

14 CD2

5 Listen and repeat.

Can you carry fifteen cans?
Can you drink them in one go?
Can you eat a hundred apples?
Can you really? Is that so?

I can't carry fifteen cans.
I can't drink them in one go.
I can't eat a hundred apples.
I'm not a hippo, no no no!

Talking about ability

6 Ask three students the questions below then tell the class.

> Marco can count to 100 in English but he can't...

The Challenge Game	Name:........... Yes No	Name:........... Yes No	Name:........... Yes No
1 Can you say the alphabet backwards?	☐ ☐	☐ ☐	☐ ☐
2 Can you count to 100 in English?	☐ ☐	☐ ☐	☐ ☐
3 Can you draw a horse?	☐ ☐	☐ ☐	☐ ☐
4 Can you dance salsa?	☐ ☐	☐ ☐	☐ ☐
5 Can you speak another language?	☐ ☐	☐ ☐	☐ ☐
6 Can you drive a car?	☐ ☐	☐ ☐	☐ ☐
7 .... (Write your own question here)	☐ ☐	☐ ☐	☐ ☐

Grammar

 ## Can for ability

1 **Read the dialogue on page 84 and complete the examples and table below.**

1 He plays the guitar, but he .... sing too.
2 I .... dance at all.

	+ / −
I / you / we / they / he / she / it	**can / can't** speak French.

Can is the same for all subjects, both singular and plural.

2 **Circle the letter of the correct sentence.**

1
   a Gregory can play the drums.
   b Gregory can't play the drums.

2
   a Mel can't drive.
   b Mel can drive.

3
   a Bryan can juggle.
   b Bryan can't juggle.

4
   a They can't walk on their hands.
   b They can walk on their hands.

5
   a She can speak French very well.
   b She can't speak French very well.

6
   a Kevin can't read braille.
   b Kevin can read braille.

3 **Complete the sentences with *can* or *can't*.**

1 I can't come now, but I .... come tomorrow.
2 I haven't got a computer, so I .... surf the web.
3 She's a really good runner – she .... run a marathon in around 3 hours.
4 My cat can't swim but it .... climb trees.
5 My little sister's three years old. She .... walk but she can't read.

 ## Can Questions and short answers

4 **Read the dialogue on page 84 and complete the table below.**

Questions

	I / you / we / they / he / she / it	see them?
1		

Short answers

✓ Yes, I / you / we / they / he / she / it **can**.
✗ Yes, I / you / we / they / he / she / it **can't**.

5 **Complete with *Can*, *can* or *can't*.**

1 .... you climb trees?
  Yes, I ....
2 .... you ride a horse?
  No, I ....
3 .... he play the piano?
  No, he ....
4 .... she speak French?
  No, she ....
5 .... they rollerblade?
  Yes, they ....
6 .... our dog swim?
  Yes, it ....

Grammar

Can for permission

6 **Complete the phrases in the table.**

[1].............. I go to the party this evening? [2].............. I see her at the weekend?	Yes, **you can**. / No, **you can't**.

7 **Match the questions and answers.**

1 Can I borrow your camera? ☐
2 Can I send an email? ☐
3 Can I come to dinner at your house? ☐
4 Can Kate stay for the weekend? ☐
5 Can I go out tonight? ☐
6 Can I close the window, please? ☐

a Sorry, I haven't got a computer.
b No, it's hot in here.
c Sorry, not tonight.
d Yes, of course. Do you like curry?
e Sorry, not now. I'm taking pictures.
f Yes, but ask her parents first.

Like / love / hate doing

8 **Read the dialogue on page 84 and complete the examples below.**

I [1].............. sing**ing** too ...
and he [2].............. listen**ing** to pop music!

He likes tell**ing** jokes.

Do you like meet**ing** up with all your family?

After the verbs **like / love / hate**, we often use verb + **ing**.

Tip

Spelling rules
· change the final 'e' to 'ing'-
  hide → hiding
· in one- syllable words, double the final
  consonant if there is a single vowel
  before it - **win → winning**

9 **Write the -ing form of the verbs.**

1 watch *watching*
2 ride ....
3 swim ....

4 go ....
5 run ....
6 rollerblade ....

10 **Complete the sentences with the -ing form of the verb in the box.**

talk   look   meet   get up   tell   sit   cycle   play   eat   walk

1 I love .... early!
2 We hate .... and waiting. It's boring!!
3 My dad likes .... at old films on TV.
4 Giulia loves .... jokes. She's very funny!
5 Do you like .... to different people?
6 They love .... their friends in town on Saturdays.
7 He hates .... meat!
8 She likes .... on her bike at weekends.
9 Does he like .... tennis at the weekend?
10 He hates .... to school.

Now do CYBER HOMEWORK 8a www.cambridge.org/elt/more

Skills

Reading

1 Read the text and circle T (True) or F (False) for the sentences below.

A Day In the Life of...

Hi! My name is Isabelle and I'm from America. I'm an acrobat. I can juggle, do tightrope-walking and unicycle and I am also a contortionist. I can sit on my head!!

I'm a member of an acrobatic group. There are 150 of us from 40 different countries. At the moment, we're in London so my hotel room is my home.

I get up at 10.55 am and order breakfast. Then I have a shower and email my friends in America and chat to them.

During my routine, I am 10 metres above the ground. There is no safety net and sometimes I'm nervous but I love performing. It's amazing. Once my routine is over, I go to the cafeteria and have dinner. I'm always hungry!

I love dancing and, after the show, I often go to a club. I sometimes go to bed at 6 am!

1	Isabelle is from Europe.	**T / F**
2	Isabclle can juggle and walk a tightrope.	**T / F**
3	There are 140 people in the acrobatic group.	**T / F**
4	At the moment, she is in London.	**T / F**
5	Isabelle gets up very early in the morning.	**T / F**
6	Isabelle's routine is on the ground.	**T / F**
7	She is sometimes nervous during a performance.	**T / F**
8	She never eats after a show.	**T / F**
9	She goes straight to bed after a show.	**T / F**
10	She always goes to bed early.	**T / F**

Listening and speaking

  CD2 15

2 Listen and tick (✓) the sports Katie can do.

| ice skating | skiing | horse riding | rollerblading | swimming | football |

3 Now ask a friend and tick or cross the pictures.

A Can you …? **B** Yes, I can. / No, I can't.

Skills

Reading and speaking

4 Complete the questionnare and see how fit you are then interview another student.

How Fit Are You?

	yes	no
1 Can you run 1 kilometre easily?	○	△
2 Can you do 20 press-ups without feeling tired?	○	△
3 Do you do exercise every day?	○	△
4 Do you walk for 30 minutes at least three times a week?	○	△
5 Do you walk or cycle to school?	○	△
6 Have you got a good pair of trainers?	○	△
7 Can you play a sport well?	○	△
8 Do you like playing sport rather than watching it?	○	△
9 Can you swim 20 lengths of the pool?	○	△
10 Are you a member of a sports team?	○	△

0–4 ○ Do more exercise. It helps you to feel good about yourself.

5–7 ○ Well done – you are quite fit. Perhaps do another sport so you can be very fit for next year!

8–10 ○ You are extremely fit ! Good for you! Keep up the good work!

Writing More connecting words

Tip | **and** – adds an idea | **but** – contrasts ideas | **so** – tells you the consequence of something

5 **a** **Read the text and circle the correct linking word.**

My name's Joe. I'm twelve years old *and* / *so* I love sports. I can swim *and* / *but* I can't dive. I can play football very well *but* / *and* I'm in the school football team. I like basketball too *and* / *but* we don't play basketball at school. I can rollerblade *and* / *but* I haven't got any rollerblades *but* / *so* I don't often go rollerblading.

b **Now write a similar text about yourself.**

 **DVD** **The Story of the Stones 4** **Rats!**

Complete the dialogue. Watch Episode 4 again to check.

Let's get out of here

Good idea

Rats

Emma	I've got an idea. You morph and then you free us.
Sarah	1.. .
Darkman	2.. !
Sarah	Well done, Daniel!
Daniel	Quick. 3.. !

CLIL Music

The orchestra

1 Read the key facts below and write the letter next to the correct word.

1 Keyboard ☐ 2 Brass ☐ 3 Percussion ☐ 4 Strings ☐ 5 Woodwind ☐

Key facts!

The word *orchestra* comes from a Greek word meaning 'dancing place'.

An orchestra has five different instrument families:

A horn , trombone, trumpet, tuba

B violin, guitar, cello, harp, viola

C recorder, flute, oboe, clarinet, saxophone

D tambourine, bell, drum, cymbals, gong, triangle

E harpsichord, piano

2 **a** Reorder the letters and write the correct words for the instruments.

1 umdr .... ☐   5 lufte .... ☐
2 hpar .... ☐   6 petrumt .... ☐
3 bymacls .... ☐   7 iartgu .... ☐
4 olvini .... ☐   8 rinetcla .... ☐

16 CD2

b Listen and tick the instruments you hear in exercise 2.

A famous composer

3 Read about Mozart and complete the notes with the dates and ages on the left.

	Wolfgang Amadeus Mozart	
6	**Born:**	January 27th, [1]......................, Salzburg, Austria
1791	**Father:**	Leopold Mozart (a musician)
35	**Age:**	5, writes his first music
1756		[2]......................, is an excellent pianist and violinist
12		7, publishes his first piece of music
		[3]......................, writes his first opera
		Writes many famous operas: *The Marriage of Figaro, The Magic Flute, Don Giovanni*, etc
		[4]......................, becomes very ill, writes his *Requiem*
		Dies in [5].................. and the *Requiem* is unfinished.

WEBQUEST

Find out about one of the Mozart operas below and do a presentationon for the class.

▪ *The Marriage of Figaro*   ▪ *The Magic Flute*   ▪ *Don Giovanni*

Check your progress 4

1 **Write the names of the clothes. [½ point each]**

1 t _ a _ _ _ _ _ 　　 4 j _ _ k _ _
2 s _ _ _ _ _ r 　　 5 t _ o _ _ _ _ _
3 s _ _ _ t 　　 6 b _ _ _ _ _

☐ **3**

2 **Reorder the letters and write the members of the family.**

1 tudhgrae 　　....................
2 rebhotr 　　....................
3 fngaahrtdre 　　....................
4 sinuco 　　....................
5 bhnsuda 　　....................
6 rtemho 　　....................

☐ **6**

3 **Complete the sentences with _is_ or _are_.**

1 The money .... on the table.
2 The shoes .... under the bed.
3 The rice .... ready.
4 The milk .... in the cup.
5 The trousers with holes .... cool!

☐ **5**

4 **Complete the questions with _can_ and write the answers.**

1 .... Harry rollerblade? ☑
....
2 .... Ben swim? ☒
....
3 .... they cook? ☒
....
4 .... she cycle? ☑
....
5 .... we speak English? ☑
....

☐ **5**

5 **Complete the questions and answers. [2 points each]**

1 .... you drive?
....
2 .... your friend dance?
....
3 How much pizza .... you eat?
....
4 .... you like skiing?
....

5 .... your friend like playing football?
....
6 .... you and your friends like going to the cinema?
....

☐ **12**

6 **Write complete sentences using the words below.**

1 They / like / juggle
....
2 We / hate / play computer games
....
3 Mum / like / rollerblade
....
4 You / love / go out
....
5 I / like / use the computer
....
6 She / hate / dance
....

☐ **6**

7 **Complete the dialogue.**

A [1]................... you swim very well?
B Yes, [2]................... .
A [3]................... your dad play the piano?
B [4] No, ...
A [5]................... your brother speak French?
B Yes, [6]................... but he [7]................... speak German.

☐ **7**

8 **Translate the questions.**

1 How much are the trainers?
....
2 How many CDs have you got?
....
3 Have you got any money?
....
4 Can she ride a horse?
....
5 Can we have pizza tonight?
....
6 Do you like reading?
....

☐ **6**

TOTAL ☐ **50**

MY PROGRESS SO FAR IS... brilliant! ☐ quite good. ☐ not great. ☐

You learn
- present continuous
- telephone numbers
- ordinal numbers
- months of the year
- dates

and then you can
- talk on the phone
- talk about birthdays
- say what people are doing

17 CD2

1 **Listen and read.**

Joe	Hello, is that the police station?
Police	Yes, it is. Who's calling?
Joe	My name's Joe. I'm phoning you about a problem in the shopping centre. A young man's running out of a music shop. Everyone's running after him. He isn't stopping! I think he's a thief. People are taking photos of him.
Police	I see … where are you calling from?
Joe	The Blue Mountain Shopping Centre. I'm standing outside the music shop, on the second floor.
Police	What's your phone number, Joe?
Joe	It's 07894 558 321.
Police	OK, a police car is going to the shopping centre now. Wait there.

(next day)

Joe	Is that today's newspaper? Perhaps the story about the thief's in it.
Adam	Let's see. Yes, it's today's date … May 7th. Here's the story: *Star Mark Diamond At The Blue Mountain Shopping Centre*! Look at the photo! He's running away from all the fans! Your thief is a famous pop star!
Joe	Oh no!

Dialogue work

2 **Read the dialogue again and circle the correct words or expressions.**

1 Joe is standing *in* / *near* the shopping centre.
2 He is talking to the police *at the police station* / *on his mobile phone*.
3 A man is running *out of* / *into* the music shop.
4 The music shop is on the *second* / *third* floor.
5 People are *taking photos of* / *writing stories about* the man.
6 Perhaps the man is a *policeman* / *thief*.
7 A police car is coming to the shopping centre *tomorrow* / *now*.
8 The next day, the story *is* / *isn't* in the newspaper.

Telephone numbers

18
CD1

3 **Listen and circle the numbers you hear.**

1 721 580 / 712 508
2 299 5043 / 299 5034
3 6619 5832 / 6119 5832

4 2305 5727 / 2350 5727
5 1682 5522 / 1682 2255
6 2867 501 / 2877 501

4 **Work in pairs and read the dialogue, then invent others.**

A Have you got *Jack's* phone number?
B Yeah, I have. Just a moment. Ready? It's *8693 2210*.
A *8693 2210*. Thanks. I'm trying to send him a text message.

Talking on the phone

5 **Work in pairs and invent dialogues using the words below.**

Tom Hi, Tom speaking.
Sandra Hi, Tom. It's Sandra here. What are you doing?
Tom I'm playing *Super Hero III*. It's great.

1 TV programmes.

I'm watching .... It's really interesting!

I'm watching .... It's boring!

2 Music.

I'm listening to .... It's great!

I'm listening to .... It's terrible!

3 Computer games.

I'm playing .... It's difficult!

I'm playing .... It's easy!

Vocabulary

Ordinal numbers

1 **Listen and repeat.**

1st	the first	9th	the ninth	17th	the seventeenth
2nd	the second	10th	the tenth	18th	the eighteenth
3rd	the third	11th	the eleventh	19th	the nineteenth
4th	the fourth	12th	the twelfth	20th	the twentieth
5th	the fifth	13th	the thirteenth	21st	the twenty-first
6th	the sixth	14th	the fourteenth	30th	the thirtieth
7th	the seventh	15th	the fifteenth		
8th	the eighth	16th	the sixteenth		

2 **Read and complete the ordinal numbers on the right.**

1 third	3........	5 twelfth	12........	9 sixth	6........
2 ninth	9........	6 tenth	10........	10 thirtieth	30........
3 second	2........	7 twenty-first	21........	11 fourteenth	14........
4 first	1........	8 eighteenth	18........	12 twentieth	20........

Months of the year

3 **Complete the months of the year.**

January
April
November
August

1	5 May	9 September
2 February	6 June	10 October
3 March	7 July	11 ....
4	8	12 December

Tip We write 'on 7th May'.
We say 'on May the seventh' or 'on the seventh of May'.

Dates

4 **Listen and tick the dates you hear.**

1 11th February ☐	4 21st December ☐	7 5th November ☐
2 12th October ☐	5 19th March ☐	8 13th January ☐
3 4th August ☐	6 2nd May ☐	9 6th June ☐

5 **Now read the dates below.**

3rd September   10th August
1st May   2nd February
4th July   21st November
30th December   19th June

Communication

Discussing dates

6 Look at the festivals below. Do you celebrate them in your country? If so, work in pairs and discuss the date for each.

Hallowe'en   Independence Day
Mother's Day   International Workers' Day / May Day
Father's Day   New Year's Day

A The 4th of July is Independence Day in America.

Yes, that's correct. / No, I think it's …

Talking about birthdays

 21 CD2

7 **a** Listen and complete the dialogue.

A How old are you, Julie?   **B** On ²............................... .
B I'm ¹............................. .   **A** What day is it this year?
A And when's your birthday?   **B** A ³............................., I think.

b Now interview four other students in the class and complete the table below.

Name	Birthday	Age	Day

Saying what people are doing

 22 CD2

8 Listen and circle what you think each person is doing.

1 **Dan**   riding a bike / playing football
2 **Conrad**   reading a text message/ skateboarding
3 **Frazer**   looking after the dog / cooking spaghetti
4 **Kate**   watching TV / playing computer games
5 **Gabby**   ice-skating / playing the piano
6 **Sherry**   sending a text message / riding a horse
7 **Dave**   riding a bike / playing tennis
8 **Chris**   watching television / using the computer
9 **Maria**   playing volleyball/ cooking
10 **Ted**   swimming / driving

Grammar

Present continuous Positive

1 **Read the dialogue on page 94 and complete the examples below.**

1 I'm .... you about a problem in the shopping centre.
2 He's .... away from all the fans!
3 People are .... photos of him.

I'm	doing some homework now.
He / She / It's	playing football at the moment.
You / We / They're	trying to find something.

Use the **Present continuous** to talk about actions happening at the moment of speaking.

2 **Circle the correct word.**

1 They *are* / *is* playing basketball.
2 I *am* / *is* walking the dog.
3 We *are* / *am* watching TV with Mum.
4 Samantha *is* / *are* riding her new bike.
5 Tamsin and Jade *are* / *is* feeding their pets.
6 Michael *is* / *am* cooking dinner in the kitchen.
7 You *are* / *is* writing a text message.
8 He *are* / *is* standing near my dad!
9 Mark and Steve *are* / *is* working together at the moment.
10 Sarah *are* / *is* running a marathon!

3 **Complete the text with the correct form of *be*.**

What ¹....................... happening in my house at the moment? Well, Dad ²....................... making lunch in the kitchen and he and Mum ³....................... talking. My brother ⁴....................... watching TV in the living room. Tilly and Twister, my two cats, ⁵....................... playing with their toys. And me? I ⁶....................... waiting for my friend to come.

4 **Complete the text with the verbs below.**

> play   skate   ride   learn   send

The children are all busy in the park today. Josie is ¹....................... basketball with her friends and Martin and John are ²....................... their bikes. Grace and Nina are ³....................... and Karen is ⁴....................... to skateboard. What's Ben doing? Oh, he's ⁵....................... another text message to Suzy! He likes Suzy! That was quick! Suzy's reading the text message right now!

5 **Complete the sentences with the verbs then match them to the correct picture.**

> riding   watching   sending
> cooking   playing   looking

a They're .... football. ☒3
b He's .... a text message. ☐
c She's .... her bike. ☐
d She's .... at her cat. ☐
e He's .... spaghetti. ☐
f They're .... TV. ☐

Grammar

Present continuous Negative

6 Read the dialogue on page 94 and complete the example below.

1 He .... stopping!

		Short form	
I'm			
He / She / It is	**not**	isn't	playing computer games right now.
		aren't	
You / We / They are			

7 Write the verbs in the negative form.

1 They're making a lot of noise.

....

2 I'm writing an essay for my English teacher.

....

3 David's travelling to France today.

....

4 He is talking to me.

....

5 They are playing football.

....

6 We are having a good time.

....

7 They are watching TV.

....

8 I'm waiting for my friend.

....

8 Complete the sentences with the negative form of *be*.

1 It .... snowing.
2 I .... sad.
3 You .... reading my book.
4 She ....watching TV.
5 He .... writing an email.
6 They .... listening to the teacher!
7 It .... working!
8 We .... playing that computer game!

Present continuous Questions and short answers

9 Read the examples and complete the table.

Am I **disturbing** you?   **No**, you **aren't**.
Are you **listening** to me?   **Yes**, I **am**.

is   am   are   isn't   aren't

Questions	Short answers	
	Positive	**Negative**
¹...................... I **disturbing** you?	Yes, you **are**.	No, you ⁴...................... .
²...................... you **listening** to me?	Yes, I **am**.	No, I'**m not**.
³...................... she **watching** TV?	Yes, she **is**.	No, she ⁵...................... .

10 Match the questions and answers.

1 **A** Tom and Cindy, are you listening to music? ☐
2 **A** Is she reading a book? ☐
3 **A** Are you watching TV, Tim? ☐
4 **A** Is Mark eating spaghetti? ☐
5 **A** Are they drinking hot chocolate? ☐
6 **A** Are you writing a message, Rita? ☐

a **B** Yes, I am.
b **B** No, I'm not.
c **B** Yes, they are.
d **B** No, we aren't.
e **B** Yes, she is.
f **B** No, he isn't.

Skills

Reading and speaking

1 Read the texts and the sentences below and circle T (True) or F (False).

Karl

I can't live without my mobile. I use it all the time. In fact, at the moment I'm sending a text. I send about 15 texts every day to my friends. I hate getting texts from my mum. It's so embarrassing. But most of all I hate not having credit. When I haven't got any credit, I can't speak to my friends and that's terrible! I've got some great pictures of my friends on my phone. This is one of my friend, James. He's sending a text message. And this is a picture of me playing with my dog. Cool!

Cheryl

I haven't got a mobile phone and I don't want one. I hate talking on the phone. My friends have all got phones and they text all the time. At the moment, my friend is talking on the phone and I'm waiting for her to stop. We're standing outside a new clothes shop in town and I want to go in and buy some new things but she is still talking!

1 Karl is sending a text.	**T / F**
2 Cheryl is standing outside a clothes shop.	**T / F**
3 Karl has got photos on his phone.	**T / F**
4 Cheryl loves talking on the phone.	**T / F**
5 Most of Cheryl's friends haven't got phones.	**T / F**
6 Karl's mum never sends him texts.	**T / F**
7 Karl always has credit.	**T / F**
8 Karl sends a lot of texts.	**T / F**

2 Work in pairs and ask and answer the questions below.

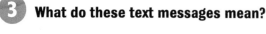

How much money do you spend on your phone every week?

Have you got a mobile phone?

How many messages do you send/receive every day?

3 What do these text messages mean?

a C U L8R = See ....

b Can U w8 4 me? = ...

c R U OK? = ...

d Gr8 2 C U ! = ...

4 Can you write other text messages in English?

Skills

Listening

5 Listen to what Caroline says and circle the correct answer.

1 How many phone calls does Caroline make?   **2 / 3**
2 Does she talk to Jude?   **Yes / No**

6 Listen again and answer the questions.

1 What is Jude's phone number? ....
2 Is Jude at home? ....
3 Are Jude and Matthew studying? ....
4 What are they doing? ....
5 Has Matthew got an MP3 player? ....
6 Who likes Caroline? ....

Writing A postcard

7 Read Tony's postcard and circle the verbs in the Present continuous.

Hi Billy,
I'm sitting in a restaurant. I'm drinking an orange juice and eating a pizza.
The food here is great!
I'm watching the people on the street.
I'm having a lot of fun. Rome is wonderful.
I love this city!
See you soon,
Tony

8 Now write your own postcard. Use the words and phrases from above.

Hi ....
I'm ....
I'm .... and ....
The .... is great.
I'm ....
I'm .... this city!
See you soon.

....

Culture

TV or not TV

80% of teens in the UK say that watching TV is one of their favourite pastimes. Over half of them say that they that would like to be a TV presenter when they grow up. Their favourite programmes are reality TV shows such as *Big Brother* and *X Factor*, and soaps such as *EastEnders* and *Neighbours*.

What are soaps?

Soaps, or soap operas, are TV and radio programmes in episodes. Most soaps follow the lives of a group of characters who live or work in the same area. Popular soaps are on television for years. You can see the characters as they grow up, get jobs, fall in and out of love, etc. The stories are usually very dramatic and every episode has a surprise event. Soap operas got their name because the first soaps had advertisements from soap companies.

Read the text quickly and find out:

the percentage of teenagers whose hobby is watching TV
....

dream jobs for more than 50% of teenagers
....

the favourite programmes of British teenagers
....

Read the words and translate them into your own language.

1 characters ....
4 surprise event ....
2 grow up ....
5 advertisements ....
3 fall in love ....

25
CD2

Now listen to Tracy from London and circle T (True) or F (False) for the sentences below.

1 Tracy is an actress in a soap opera. T / F
2 Tracy studies soap operas at school. T / F
3 The class discusses the theme of the soap opera. T / F
4 They watch lots of different soap operas. T / F
5 Not many young people watch soap operas. T / F
6 Tracy thinks that studying soap operas is a good idea. T / F

What do you think?

A new invention called Square-eyes will encourage young people to do exercise by giving them extra time watching TV. You simply put Square-eyes into your shoe and it records how many steps you take in a day. Square-eyes then sends the information to the television and it calculates how much watching time you have earned. The more you walk the more TV you can watch in the evening.

MORE! Online Action Box Listening and Quiz online.
Write a text for the MORE! Online journal. **Put it online for students from other countries to read.**

Go to www.cambridge.org/elt/more for extra CULTURE

UNIT 10 I'm surfing the web!

You learn
- articles
- present simple vs. present continuous
- words for free-time activities and computers

and then you can
- make invitations
- talk about your free time

27 CD2

1 Listen and read.

Adam Hi, Kelly, what are you doing? Are you playing computer games again?

Kelly No, I don't always play computer games! Right now, I'm surfing the web! But I've got a problem with my computer. I can't print this page …

Adam Let me see. Are you sure the printer cable is connected to the computer?

Kelly Yes, but it still isn't working.

Adam Well, there's something wrong with your printer then. Send it to me by email. Then come to my house and we can print it out there. I can download some new music too. We can watch a DVD or something later if you want.

Kelly OK … hold on, look at this. There's no paper in the printer tray!

Adam Silly you! You need to fill it up!

Kelly Yes, I know!

Dialogue work

2 **Match the sentence halves.**

1 Kelly is	a print the page.
2 Kelly doesn't always	b surfing the web.
3 Kelly can't	c something wrong with the printer.
4 Adam thinks there is	d play computer games.
5 Kelly needs	e to add paper to the printer.

Making invitations

3 **Work in pairs and practise the dialogue, then invent new ones.**

A What are you doing right now?

B *I'm surfing the web and listening to music.*

A Can you come over to my place?

B Why? What's going on?

A *Steve and I are playing a computer game.*

4 **a** **Listen and circle the correct words, then listen again and repeat.**

1 **Jim** Would you like to come to the ¹*match / cinema* with me this evening?

   Sue I'd love to.

   Jim Shall we meet at ²*school / the youth club*?

   Sue Sure. Let's meet there at ³*7 pm / 8 pm*.

2 **Mel** Would you like to go for a ⁴*bike ride / run*?

   Mark Sorry, I can't.

   Mel What about tomorrow?

   Mark OK, let's go in the morning at about ⁵*9 / 11*.

   Mel OK, great!

b **Invent new dialogues using the other words.**

Vocabulary

Computers

1 Complete the expressions with the words on the left.

burn	1 to *create* a backup of your files
check	2 to .... your hard disk for viruses
click	3 to .... an email to a friend
~~create~~	4 to .... your files on your hard disk
run	5 to .... a program
save	6 to .... with a mouse
send	7 to .... the web
surf	8 to .... a CD

Free time activities

2 Write the correct expression under the picture.

have a pizza   meet friends   have an ice cream   go for a run   walk the dog   go rollerblading
go skateboarding   exercise in the gym   go swimming   go for a walk   play football   go for a bike ride

....

....

....

....

....

....

....

....

....

....

....

....

....

....

....

....

....

....

....

....

....

....

....

....

Communication

Sounds right /w/

3 **Listen and repeat.**

We can hang out **w**ith friends,
We can **w**atch TV,
We can **w**alk, **w**e can talk –
Have a **w**eekend with me!

Talking about your free time

4 **Ask and answer in pairs.**

What do you like doing in your free time?
How often do you do it?
How much time do you spend on it?
Who do you do it with?

an hour a day / two hours a week
once a month / every day
my friend(s) / my brother / on my own

5 **Complete the questionnaire, then interview
your partner.**

Are you a Computer Whizzkid?

1	Are you connected to the web at the moment?	✓	✗
2	Do you spend more than 3 hours on your computer each day?	✓	✗
3	Do you play a lot of computer games?	✓	✗
4	Can you upload music and photos?	✓	✗
5	Have you got your own blog?	✓	✗
6	Can you make links from one page to another?	✓	✗
7	Can you use more than 10 computer software programs?	✓	✗
8	Can you fix your computer when it goes wrong?	✓	✗
9	Do you watch films on a computer?	✓	✗
10	Are you on any social networks at the moment?	✓	✗

1–3	✓	You are not a computer whizzkid and probably don't like computers and technology that much.
4–7	✓	You are a bit of a computer whizzkid and use your computer sometimes but not all the time.
8–10	✓	You are a computer whizzkid!

Grammar

Articles

1 **Read the examples and complete the rules below.**

> Steve and I are playing a computer game.
>
> How often do you run an anti-virus program?
>
> There's something wrong with the hard disk.
>
> The indefinite articles are **a** and **an**.
>
> [1]................. is used before nouns that begin with a consonant.
>
> [2]................. is used before nouns that begin with a vowel sound.
>
> The definite article is **the**.

2 **Complete the sentences with *a*, *an* or –.**

1 She's having .... lunch with her friends.
2 Look! There's .... ice cream bar!
3 He lives in .... old house.
4 She is working in .... company in the centre of town.
5 I'm phoning .... man from Italy.
6 They're eating .... hamburger with cheese.

3 **Circle the correct answer.**

1 I am surfing *a / the* web.
2 Have you got *an / the* laptop?
3 She is fixing *a / an* old computer.
4 We are washing *an / the* car.
5 They are having *a / an* pizza.
6 He is walking *an / the* dog.

4 **Complete the sentences with *a*, *an* or *the*.**

1 .... theatre in our town is closed on Sundays!
2 That's .... great film!
3 He's got .... orange computer!
4 .... house at the end of the road is my grandma's.
5 .... man who lives opposite us is my Maths teacher.
6 It's .... portable laptop, not .... tablet!

Present simple vs. present continuous

> What **are** you do**ing** right now?
>
> I**'m** look**ing** at the computer.
>
> Steve and I **are** play**ing** computer games.
>
> How often **do** you **run** an anti-virus program?
>
> I **don't** eat meat.
>
> He often wear**s** jeans.
>
> **Does** she like tennis?
>
> I only **read** about TV programmes.

5 **Study the examples and complete the rules with the Present simple or Present continuous.**

To talk about habit, routines and general information, we use the [1]........................ .

To talk about what's happening at the moment of speaking we use the [2]........................ .

We always use the verb **be** in the Present [3]........................ .

We use **do** and **does** to make questions in the Present [4]........................ .

We use **don't** and **doesn't** to make negative sentences in the Present [5]........................ .

We add an **–s** to the third person singular in the Present [6]........................ .

Grammar

6 **Complete the sentences with the Present simple or the Present continuous.**

1 Brian usually .... the computer to do his homework. (use)

2 I'm lost. I .... to find Tim's house. (try)

3 .... you .... to come to the cinema with us? (want)

4 Iris .... a very good day today! (not have)

5 The teacher always .... we're good students. (say)

6 .... you .... for the bus? (wait)

7 **What are these people doing? Look at the photos and write questions and answers.**

Janice

Mike

Ted

Jake & Tim

Joe

Jill & Jack

1 Janice / rollerblading
   Is Janice rollerblading?
   No, she's walking the dog.

2 Mike / swimming
   ....?
   ....

3 Ted / skateboarding
   ....?
   ....

4 Jake and Tim / meeting friends
   ....?
   ....

5 Joe / swimming
   ....?
   ....

6 Jill and Jack / having an ice cream
   ....?
   ....

8 **Circle the correct sentence.**

1 **a** Mum washes her hair at the moment.
   b Mum's washing her hair at the moment.

2 **a** I spend a weekend in the country.
   b I'm spending a weekend in the country

3 **a** Ben is sometimes staying at our house.
   b Ben sometimes stays at our house.

4 **a** Are you working at the moment?
   b Are you work at the moment?

5 **a** Sheena is liking living in Scotland.
   b Sheena likes living in Scotland.

6 **a** I'm printing this essay.
   b I print this essay.

Now do CYBER HOMEWORK 10a www.cambridge.org/elt/more

Skills

Reading

1 **Read the texts. Then read the sentences below and write the name of the person they refer to.**

1 She is wearing a T-shirt with an owl on it. ....

2 He takes photos of graffiti art. ....

3 She's got sixty key rings. ....

4 He is making a poster. ....

5 She is looking for a particular type of key ring. ....

6 She is choosing photos. ....

Mark

I collect photos of graffiti.

I take the photos on my mobile phone. I stick all the photos together on my laptop. Then I make posters of graffiti art and I give them to my friends. Today I am making a poster for my sister. She is choosing the photos at the moment.

I collect key rings. Sarah

I've got sixty key rings in my collection. Today I'm in a gift shop. I'm looking for a key ring with a zebra on it. I love zebras. I make my own key rings too. I've got a beautiful one with different coloured beads.

Grace

I collect owls.

I love Harry Potter's snowy owl, Hedwig. Every time I go to a new place, I buy an owl. I've got lots of different things with owls on them. I've got a mug with an owl on it, a T-shirt with an owl on it and a bracelet with an owl on it. I am wearing my owl T-shirt now. My friend Hermione is wearing an owl bracelet.

Listening

30 CD2

2 **Listen to what Robbie is doing at the moment and circle T (True) or F (False).**

1	Robbie is playing a computer game on his tablet now.	T / F
2	Robbie uploads music for his friends.	T / F
3	He is uploading some music now.	T / F
4	Jake and Lucas are playing volleyball in the photo.	T / F
5	Robbie's sister rides a bike.	T / F
6	Robbie's friend Lucas is calling him now.	T / F

Skills

Speaking

3 What do you do on your computer/tablet/phone? Tick the boxes for you. Then ask a friend.

	Me	My friend
download music and films?	☐	☐
call friends?	☐	☐
play online games?	☐	☐
post photos on social networks?	☐	☐
research projects?	☐	☐
do homework?	☐	☐
blog?	☐	☐

A Do you …?

B Yes, I do. / No, I don't.

Writing Describing a hobby

4 Read the text, then write about your own hobby or the hobby of a friend.

My hobby is collecting tea bags. I have a large collection from all over the world. Every time my dad or friends go away on holiday, I ask them to bring back different ones for me. They are all lovely colours. I like looking at them. I have over 5000 in my collection now.

My hobby / My friend's hobby is ....
I have / She / He has ....
....
....
....

The Story of the Stones 5 Two more to go!

Complete the dialogue. Watch Episode 5 again to check.

Oh, come on
I'm not sure
be careful
Just a minute

Emma .... This message is from …?

Daniel I don't know. Sunborn I guess – but ....

Emma I'm sure it's a trap. Let's not go!

Sarah .... We're fast. We're strong. We're clever. What do you think, Daniel?

Daniel I'm not sure … Remember the net! Remember Darkman! He's bad and he's clever.

Sarah Listen. I can fly. Nothing can happen to me. I want to check it out, OK?

Emma OK. But Sarah – .... !

CLIL Technology

Mobiles!

1 **Where are all the old mobile phones?**
Read the key facts below and find out.

Key facts!

- There are six billion mobile phones in use in the world today.
- That's more than ten billion mobiles in the world since 1994.
- Many people change their mobiles every 12-18 months, even if the phone works well.
- Only 5% of people recycle their old phones.

A What can I do with my old mobile phone?
B Does it work?
A Yes.
B You can sell it. Give it to your family, a friend or a charity. Recycle it or keep it in a drawer.

C What can I do with my old mobile phone?
B Does it work?
C No.
B You can keep it in a drawer. Sell it. Give it to a charity or recycle, but please don't it throw it in the bin.
C What happens if I give it to a charity?
B Some phones are given to people who need them, others are sold for recycling. Most of the chemicals can be used again to make new phones!
C What happens if I throw my phone in the bin?
B It will go to landfill and the chemicals in it will leak into the water in the ground!
C What chemicals? Isn't a phone just plastic and metal?
B No!

31 CD2 **2** **What is inside a mobile phone?**
Listen and tick (✓) the boxes below.

plastic ☐	lithium (Li) ☐	glass ☐	chromium (Cr) ☐
paper ☐	lead (Pb) ☐	wood ☐	mercury (Hg) ☐
		nickel (Ni) ☐	cadmium (Cd) ☐

3 **Discuss with a partner.**

1 Do you ever use a mobile? What do you do with it?
2 How many times do you use a mobile in one day?

WEBQUEST

Find out:
- Where can you sell or give away old mobile phones near your home?
- How are modern mobile phones different from the first mobiles?

 Go to www.cambridge.org/elt/more for extra CLIL

Check your progress 5

1 Write the ordinal numbers. [½ point each]

1 12th ....
2 4th ....
3 1st ....
4 23rd ....
5 2nd ....
6 21st ....

☐ **3**

2 Write the computer words.

1 b _ _ _ a disk
2 s _ _ _ the web
3 r _ _ a program
4 c _ _ _ _ _ a file
5 c _ _ _ _ on the mouse
6 e _ _ _ _ some text
7 s _ _ _ to the hard disk

☐ **7**

3 Complete the questions in the Present continuous. Use the verbs in brackets.

1 .... he .... a horse? (ride)
2 .... we .... English? (study)
3 .... she .... an email? (write)
4 .... they .... in the sea? (swim)
5 .... I .... to music? (listening)

☐ **5**

4 Match the answers to the questions in exercise 3.

a .... Yes, I am.
b .... No, we aren't.
c .... Yes, she is.
d .... Yes, they are.
e .... No, he isn't.

☐ **5**

5 Write questions and answers in the Present continuous. [2 points each]

1 Jenny / eat pizza ☒ / eat pasta ☑

....

2 Your brother / play the piano ☒ / play the guitar ☑

....

3 Mark and Lucy / swim ☒ / cycle ☑

....

4 You and Tony / go to the park ☒ / go to the stadium ☑

....

5 They / drink milk ☒ / drink hot chocolate ☑

....

6 I / read ☒ / sleep ☑

....

☐ **12**

6 Circle the correct sentence.

1 a They are running now.
   b They run now.
2 a She sends emails every day.
   b She is sending emails every day.
3 a We read a book at the moment.
   b We are reading a book at the moment.
4 a Ellie and Kirsten play tennis at the moment.
   b Ellie and Kirsten are playing tennis at the moment.
5 a I do my homework now.
   b I am doing my homework now.
6 a You eat pizza every Sunday.
   b You are eating pizza every Sunday.

☐ **6**

7 Complete the dialogue.

A ¹.......................... Jack .... every week? (swim)
B Yes, ².......................... .
A ³.......................... he .... at the moment? (swim)
B ⁴ No, ...
A ⁵ What .... he ....? (do)
B He ⁶.......................... .... (watch TV)

☐ **6**

8 Translate the questions and sentences.

1 Are you phoning your mum?

....

2 They are travelling to London now.

....

3 Does she live in France?

....

4 He is wearing a blue T-shirt.

....

5 Are you eating an ice cream?

....

6 Is your friend playing with her dog?

....

☐ **6**

TOTAL ☐ **50**

MY PROGRESS SO FAR IS... brilliant! ☐   quite good. ☐   not great. ☐

You learn
- past simple of *be*
- past time expressions
- words for furniture
- prepositions (revision)

and then you can
- say where people were
- say where things are

1 Listen and read.

Leah is staying at Adam's house for a few nights while her parents are away. But, there is a problem...

Mum Adam, were you in the kitchen last night?

Adam No, I wasn't. Why?

Mum There were four chocolates in the fridge last night. They were in blue paper. Now there's only one left. Where were you last night?

Adam I was in bed, Mum! First I was here in the living room. You were with me, remember?

Mum Yes, that film was on TV. But it was over at 9.

Adam I was in the shower after that. Then it was bedtime. Maybe it was Dad.

He wasn't in the living room last night...

Leah I was on the computer last night at 8.30. There was an email from Celine. I was in my room at 9.

Mum Well, there was some blue paper next to the computer this morning. It was from the missing chocolates!

Adam Sorry, I was hungry, Mum.

Mum Adam! The chocolates weren't for you!

Adam But they were delicious, Mum...

Dialogue work

2 **Read the dialogue again and circle T (True) or F (False) below.**

1 There was a film on TV last night. **T / F**

2 Adam was in the living room from 8 to 9. **T / F**

3 Leah was on the computer at 8.30. **T / F**

4 There were four chocolates in the fridge this morning. **T / F**

5 There was some blue paper next to the computer this morning. **T / F**

3 **Listen and repeat.**

A Where was Leah yesterday evening?

B She was in the bedroom.

A Where were Mum and Adam at 8.30?

B They were in the living room.

Saying where people were

4 **Listen and match the people to the correct places. Write the number next to the name.**

☐ Mark   ☐ Meg   ☐ Paul   ☐ Sally   ☐ Zach   ☐ Emma

5 **Work with a partner and check your answers.**

A Sally was at the cinema yesterday evening.

B Correct. / No, she wasn't. She was at the …

6 **Say where you were yesterday and at other times last week.**

A I was in the park with my friends *yesterday* / *on Saturday* / *last Sunday.*

B I was…

Vocabulary

Furniture (revision)

  1 Write the correct names under the photos, then listen and check.

lamp
cupboard
armchair
sink
curtains
wardrobe
radiator
bed
cooker
rug
table
fridge
bedside table
carpet
chair
sofa

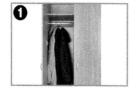

1 ....

2 ....

3 ....

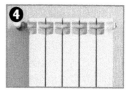

4 ....

5 ....

6 ....

7 ....

8 ....

9 ....

10 ....

11 ....

12 ....

13 ....

14 ....

15 ....

16 ....

Prepositions (revision)

2 Where is the cat and the objects below? Write the correct preposition under the picture.

in
above
under
behind
on
in front of
between
next to

vase
1 ....

cat
2 ....

picture
3 ....

cat
4 ....

cat
5 ....

cat
6 ....

vases
7 ....

cat
8 ....

Communication

Saying where things are

3 **Work in pairs. Ask your partner questions about objects in his/her bedroom and write a list.**

A Is there a clock on your bedside table?

B Yes, there is. / No, there isn't.

Sounds right   *was / were*

36 CD2

4 **Listen and repeat.**

I was hot!

He was happy.	I wasn't happy.	Was he happy?
I was hot.	I was sad.	Yes, he was.
She was happy.	They were happy.	Were you happy?
I was not.	I was mad.	No, because…

Saying where things were

5 **Look at the two photos of the room and talk about the differences between yesterday and today.**

Yesterday, there was a lamp on the cupboard.

Yesterday

Today

Grammar

🔍 Past simple of *be*
Positive and negative

1 Look at the sentences from the dialogue on page 114.

Adam First, I was in the living room.

Mum There were four chocolates in the fridge last night.

Adam He wasn't in the living room last night.

Mum The chocolates weren't for you!

Now complete the table.

Positive	Negative
I [1].................... in the living room.	I wasn't in the kitchen. (was not)
You were at home.	You weren't with him. (were not)
He was in his bedroom.	He [5].................... with us. (was not)
She [2].................... with me.	She wasn't in her bedroom. (was not)
It was on the fridge.	It [6].................... in your bedroom. (was not)
We were in the living room.	We weren't at home. (were not)
You [3].................... in the bedroom.	You [7].................... at home. (were not)
They [4].................... in the kitchen.	They [8].................... alone. (were not)

2 Complete the text with *was* or *were*.

Anna [1].................... at home all day on Sunday.

At 2 o'clock, Anna and her family [2].................... in the kitchen, eating. They [3].................... hungry.

Anna and her brother [4].................... in the living room at 9 pm. Anna [5].................... tired, so at 9.30 she [6].................... in bed – asleep!

3 Where was Ken? Reorder the words to make sentences.

1 room / He / in / his / was / .

....

2 was / on / He / to / phone / Mike / the / .

....

3 the / park / were / Mike / at / He / and / .

....

4 Mike / were / He / at / and / cinema / the / .

....

4 Circle the correct verb.

At 6 pm, I [1] *was / were* at home with my sister. We [2] *weren't / wasn't* alone – our mum [3] *was / weren't* there. Dad [4] *wasn't / were* there – he [5] *was / were* at work. My sister and I [6] *were / was* hungry!

5 Look at the picture. Complete the sentences with the positive or the negative form.

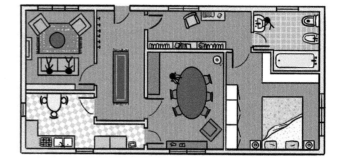

1 Mrs Lodge .... (✓) with her sister in the sitting room.

2 Mr Lodge .... (✗) in the library with his wife.

3 Mr Lodge .... (✗) with his wife at 7 pm.

4 Mr Lodge .... (✓) in the dining room.

5 Bobby .... (✗) with his dad.

6 Bobby .... (✓) in the bathroom.

Grammar

Past simple of be
Questions and short answers

6 **Look at the sentences below.**

Adam, **were** you in the kitchen last night?
No, I **wasn't**.
Was the football game on TV yesterday?
Yes, it **was**.

Now complete the table.

Questions	Short answers	
	Positive	Negative
Was I late?	Yes, I was.	No, I wasn't.
Were you in my room?	Yes, you 1.................... .	No, you weren't.
Was he in my room?	Yes, he was.	No, he 6.................... .
Was she in my room?	Yes, she 2.................... .	No, she 7.................... .
Was it cold?	Yes, it 3.................... .	No, it 8.................... .
Were we late?	Yes, we were.	No, we weren't.
Were you late?	Yes, you 4.................... .	No, you 9.................... .
Were they late?	Yes, they 5.................... .	No, they 10.................... .

7 **Match the questions and answers.**

1 Where were you at 9 pm? ☐
2 Was your mum in the kitchen? ☐
3 Where was your dad? ☐
4 Were you in the living room at 6 pm? ☐
5 Where were your sisters? ☐
6 Were you and Nick hungry? ☐

a He was in the library.
b I was in my bedroom.
c Yes, we were.
d No, I wasn't.
e Yes, she was.
f They were in the dining room.

8 **Complete the questions and answers.**

1 **A** Where .... you at 9 pm?
  B I was in my bedroom.
2 **A** Was your mum in the kitchen?
  B Yes, she ....
3 **A** .... was your dad?
  B He was in the library.
4 **A** Were you in the living room at 6 pm?
  B No, I ....
5 **A** Where .... your sisters?
  B They were in the dining room.
6 **A** Were you and Nick hungry?
  B No, we ....

Past time expressions

You were there **yesterday evening**.
Where were you **at 5 o'clock**?
Where were you **from 6 to 9**?
Last Sunday I was at a football game.
I was not at home **yesterday**.

9 **Reorder the words to make sentences.**

1 late/ I / morning / was / yesterday / .
....
....

2 They / at / last / Tuesday / were / school / .
....
....

3 We / at / gym / the / were / from 7 to 9 / .
....
....

4 He / there / wasn't / 8 o'clock / at / .
....
....

Skills

Listening

1 **Listen and match the people to the correct rooms.**

1 Lady Grant is in
2 The cook is in
3 Percy is in
4 Lucinda is in
5 Lord Grant is in
6 Tom Barrymore is in

a the kitchen.
b the living room.
c the library.
d the bathroom.
e the bedroom.
f the dining room.

Reading

2 **Read the story *Teacups* and circle T (True) or F (False) for the sentences below. Correct the false sentences.**

'Give me your notes, Jenkins.'
'Of course, Inspector.'
'Now let's look at these notes again. Hmmm. The butler was in the kitchen from 8.30 pm to 10 pm, but he wasn't in the living room. And he wasn't in his bedroom.
The maid was in the library from 8 pm to 10 pm, cleaning the fireplace for the next day.
The cook wasn't there at all. She was at home with her sick daughter.
Mr and Mrs Strong were in the living room drinking tea at 8.30 pm. And their daughter Sara was with them. Good. At 9 pm, Mrs Strong was in her bedroom. And, at 10 pm, she was dead. On the floor, there was a knife and a cup of tea.'
'All my notes are correct, Inspector.'
'Yes, I can see that, Jenkins. Very good. I think we can arrest the butler now.'
'But why the butler, sir?'
'I don't think he's telling the truth. All those teacups, Jenkins – and he was in the kitchen all the time? It's the butler's job to serve them tea. I don't believe him. Go and arrest him.'

1 The butler was in the kitchen from 8.30 pm to 10 pm.   **T / F**
2 The maid was in the library at 7 pm.   **T / F**
3 The cook wasn't there.   **T / F**
4 Mr and Mrs Strong were in the living room at 10 pm.   **T / F**
5 Sara Strong was in the living room at 8.30 pm.   **T / F**
6 At 9 pm, Mrs Strong was in her bedroom.   **T / F**

Skills

Listening and speaking

38 CD2 **3** Listen and read the dialogue, then interview three students in your class and compare answers.

Martin   Hi, *Nora*, where were you yesterday?

Nora   I was *at the football match.*

Martin   Really? How was it?

Nora   *Brilliant.* And where were you?

Martin   I was *at home, doing homework.*

Nora   Oh. *Poor you!*

Writing Using time markers

Tip   Time prepositions
Use **at** with times (at 5 o'clock)
From and **to** with a period of time (from Monday to Friday)
On with days of the week (on Sunday)
Until about a length of time. (I was there until 10.00)

4 Read the text and circle the time prepositions.

Last Sunday, Noreen was at home. She was in bed until 11 o'clock.

At 1 pm, she was in the kitchen with her family for lunch.

Noreen was in the park with her dog from 2.30 to 4 pm.

She was back home at 4.30 pm.

At 7 o'clock, Noreen was in the living room.

At 9.30, she was in bed again. She was tired!

5 Write a text about yourself.

Last Sunday, I was ....

Then, ...

From .... to .... , I was ....

At .... o'clock ....

At .... o'clock ....

Culture

a

British history

Read the texts and match them to the correct photo.

☐ **Hadrian's Wall** is in the north of England. The Romans built it to keep the Scots out of Roman Britain. The Romans came to Britain in 43 AD and built many cities such as London, Bath and Chester. The suffixes *–chester* (Manchester) and *–caster* (Lancaster) come from the Latin word for camp (castra).

☐ **Westminster Palace** is the official name of the Houses of Parliament, where the British Government meets. It became a Royal Palace after The Norman Conquest of Britain in 1066. The Palace has a clock tower, with London's most famous bell: Big Ben.

☐ **Stonehenge** is one of the most famous and mysterious places in Britain. No-one knows when it was built or who built it. Some experts think it dates to 4000 BC, when farmers built it for ceremonies.

☐ **Stratford-upon-Avon** was the home of Britain's most famous author, William Shakespeare. It is a typical Elizabethan town. Over 2 million tourists come to the small town every year to visit Shakespeare's home. Shakespeare wrote 37 plays and 154 poems before he died, aged 52, in 1616. His most famous plays include *Romeo and Juliet*, *Hamlet* and *Macbeth*.

b

c

d

39
CD1

Listen and say which places Anne and Paul are visiting.

They are visiting

....

....

....

MORE! Online Action Box

Listening and Quiz online.
Write a text for the MORE! Online journal. Put it online for students from other countries to read.

> Go to www.cambridge.org/elt/more for extra CULTURE

Extra Reading

INTERNATIONAL CRIME BUSTERS EUROPE

The International Crime Busters are flying into Oslo.

So, what's the problem in Norway?

A snow monster. It's scaring people in a small village in the North.

So we aren't stopping in Oslo.

That's right. We're going to take another small aeroplane to the Arctic Circle.

1

Wow! The Northern lights!

They're so beautiful. They're incredible.

2

The attacks started a month ago – always at night. The people are really scared. Many are leaving the village.

Do you have any photos of this monster?

No, but I can show you some footprints. Follow me.

3

Here you are.

Wow. They're big!

Well, there's only one thing to do. Let's follow them.

4

The footprints are going into this cave. Let's go in.

Not me. I'm going back to the town. Good luck.

Looks like we're on our own, Nick.

5

I don't think we'll find any monsters in that cave.

Why not?

Because what came out of that cave was human, I'm sure. Look!

6

Well, here's our monster.

Let's wait and see who comes to get this tonight.

But, let's get the police chief back first.

7

Later that night.

Stop right there!

8

So, he's working for the oil company.

Yes, they want to drill for oil here but they can't because of the people who live here.

So, they used this 'monster' to scare the people away.

That's right. But thanks to the ICB, their plan failed!

9

You learn
- past simple
- places to go
- words for things to do

and then you can
- say when you were somewhere
- find out information

  1 **Listen and read.**

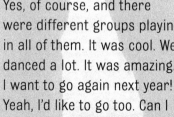

Kelly Hi, Dave! You weren't at the party on Saturday. Were you away?

Dave Yes, I was on the Isle of Wight for three days with Mum and Dad. There was a great music festival there. There were more than 50 thousand people!

Kelly Wow! What was it like?

Dave It was fantastic! Of course, it rained! You know what summer is like in England!

Kelly Of course!! Were you in a hostel?

Dave No, we camped in a field. It was fun. The campsite was very well organised. There was one site where people put up your tent for you which was very helpful! I'm not very good with tents!

Kelly No, neither am I! Were there places to eat?

Dave Yes, of course, and there were different groups playing in all of them. It was cool. We danced a lot. It was amazing. I want to go again next year!

Kelly Yeah, I'd like to go too. Can I come with you?

Dave Sure!

Dialogue work

2 Read the sentences and circle T (True) or F (False).

1 Dave was ill on Saturday.	**T / F**
2 He was with his uncle.	**T / F**
3 Dave was on the Isle of Wight for three days.	**T / F**
4 The weather was good.	**T / F**
5 They camped.	**T / F**
6 Dave wants to go again.	**T / F**
7 Kelly doesn't want to go to the festival.	**T / F**

Saying when you were somewhere

3 Look at the pictures and say where Enrique was. Use expressions like ... *hours / months ago, yesterday evening, last year,* etc.

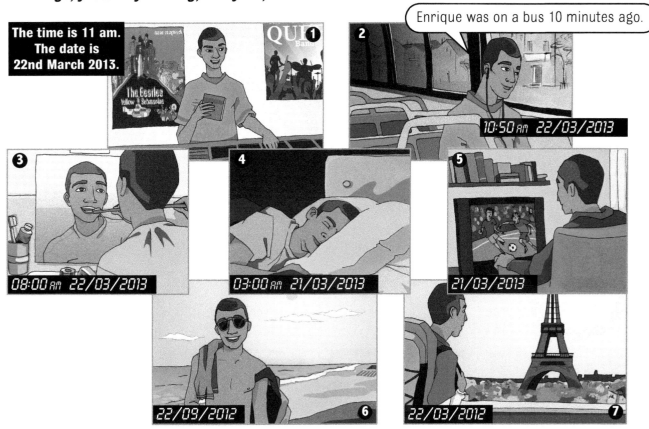

The time is 11 am. The date is 22nd March 2013. **①**

② Enrique was on a bus 10 minutes ago.

10:50 AM 22/03/2013

③ 08:00 AM 22/03/2013

④ 03:00 AM 21/03/2013

⑤ 21/03/2013

22/09/2012 **⑥**

22/03/2012 **⑦**

4 **a** Work in pairs. Ask and answer questions with your partner.

10 minutes   2 hours   8 hours   2 days
1 week   1 year

A Where were you 10 minutes ago?

B I was at lunch!

b Discuss your answers with the class. Were any of you in the same places at the same time?

Vocabulary

Things to do

1 Write the words under the correct photos, then listen and check.

caving
snorkelling
biking
hiking
camping
scuba diving
climbing
kayaking

....

 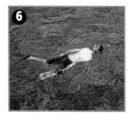  

....

2 Look at the equipment below and say which sport you use it for.

A You use a *rope* for climbing.

rope	wetsuit, aqualung and fins	hiking boots
bike and helmet	tent and sleeping bag	and backpack
kayak and paddle	snorkel, mask	

Places to go

3 Match the words to the photos.

1 theme park	4 art gallery	7 theatre
2 restaurant	5 monument	8 river
3 museum	6 show	

Communication

Sounds right /t/ /d/ /ɪd/

 4 **Listen and repeat.**

/t/
1 She walked to the park.
2 We looked at the photos.
3 They danced all night.

/d/
4 We listened to CDs.
5 I loved the music.
6 He played the piano.

/ɪd/
7 He needed some money.
8 It started to rain.
9 She hated the film.

5 **a** **Look at the pictures of this young boy and complete the sentences below. Use verbs from exercise 4.**

When I was ten, I .... dancing.
I .... playing with my train.
I .... to school.

Now, I love dancing, I hate playing with my train and I drive to school!!

b **Think of more sentences beginning with *When I was ten, ...* and tell the class.**

Finding out information

 6 **Stephen wants to try scuba diving.**
Listen and complete the dialogue.

Stephen	Hi. ¹........................... is a scuba diving lesson?
Assistant	It's ²........................... per hour.
Stephen	OK. What do I need ?
Assistant	Just your swimming costume. We provide the equipment and ³........................... . Is it your first time?
Stephen	Yes, it is. What time do the lessons ⁴...........................?
Assistant	Well, the beginner's course starts on ⁵........................... at 8 pm in the swimming pool. You need to complete this form. There are ⁶........................... lessons in total.
Stephen	OK, how much does it cost?
Assistant	It's ⁷........................... for the complete course.
Stephen	OK, thank you!

b **Work in pairs and invent similar dialogues for other sports courses.**

Grammar

🔍 Past simple regular verbs Positive

1 Complete the sentences with these words.

> scored   played   finished   wanted

1 I .... for the school team.
2 The game .... about an hour ago.
3 We really .... to win.
4 I .... a goal.

2 Complete the rule.

To use regular verbs in the past tense we add -[1]........... to the end of the verb.
If the verb ends in **-e**, then we just add -[2]........... .
If the verb ends in consonant **+y** we change the **-y** to [3].......... and add.[4]........... .

3 Write the Past simple forms of these verbs.

walk	....	look	....
wait	....	open	....
love	....	like	....
relax	....	hate	....
watch	....	live	....
listen	....	play	....
surf	....	borrow	....
close	....	arrive	....
touch	....	happen	....
climb	....	dance	....
talk	....	phone	....
hurry	....	try	....
study	....		

Jennifer phoned for help.

4 Circle the Past simple forms of the verbs in the text below then complete the table.

Yesterday I played football. At 6 o'clock it started to rain. So I phoned my friend Daniel. We listened to some CDs and then watched a great film on TV. At 10, Daniel's father arrived. Daniel wanted to see the ending of the film. He asked his father of that was OK. Fortunately, it was!

Present	Past
....	....
....	....
....	....
....	....
....	....
....	....
....	....
....	....

5 Complete the sentence with the Past simple form of the verbs.

1 Mr Miller's dog .... a cat. (chase)
2 Dad .... at 7 pm. (arrive)
3 The dog .... into the water. (jump)
4 I .... to music all evening. (listen)
5 Sarah .... me at 9. (phone)
6 I .... Annie's schoolbag. (carry)

6 Complete the text with the Past simple form of the verbs below.

> be (x5)   look (x3)   turn   open   (not) be

The alarm clock rang. I [1]...................... at it – it [2]...................... 5 am.
I [3]...................... it off. A few minutes later, it rang again. I [4]...................... at it – it [5]...................... 4.45 am! Then there [6]...................... a strange noise. Something [7]...................... in the garden. I [8]...................... the window. I [9]...................... out. This [10]...................... my garden! Where [11]...................... I?

Grammar

7 Complete the story with the Past simple of the verbs below.

to be (x3)
shout
rescue
walk
stay
happen
want

Last Saturday something bad [1]........................ .
We [2]........................ at the sea. The sea [3]........................
warm that day. I can't swim but I [4]........................ to
go into the water. I [5]........................ into the sea alone.
My friends [6]........................ on the beach. Suddenly,
the water [7]........................ very deep. 'Help, help, I
can't swim,' I [8]........................ Of course, my friends
[9]........................ me. Now I'm having swimming
lessons!

8 Circle the correct answers to complete the text.

Yesterday, [1]........................ my birthday. My friends and
I [2]........................ in the park [3]........................ the morning.
Then we [4]........................ some food so we [5]........................
to my house. Mum and Dad weren't there, so I
[6]........................ them. 'Can you come home? My friends
and I are hungry!' They [7]........................ home ten
minutes later and [8]........................ us a great meal!

1 **A** on	3 **A** at	5 **A** was	7 **A** were
B is	**B** in	**B** were	**B** is
C was	**C** on	**C** walked	**C** arrived
2 **A** was	4 **A** wanted	6 **A** those	8 **A** cooked
B are	**B** were	**B** phoned	**B** watched
C played	**C** shouted	**C** them	**C** liked

9 Complete the text with the verbs below.

was   chased   watched   tried   jumped   were

My friend and I [1]........................ a DVD yesterday evening.
It [2]........................ about a bank robbery. The robber
[3]........................ out of the bank window and [4]........................
to run away. But the police [5]........................ the robber.
And they [6]........................ surprised when they found out it
was a child!!

Now do CYBER HOMEWORK 12a www.cambridge.org/elt/more

Skills

Reading

1 Read the story and circle T (True) or F (False) for the sentences below.

My name is Mark and I was on an adventure holiday last month. I love scuba diving so I decided to book a dive with the local diving school.

My instructor helped me to put on my aqualungs, my own old mask and fins and showed me the depth gauge where you can see how much oxygen is in the tanks.

I dived under the waves behind the instructor. It was incredible – so many different fish and such beautiful colours! I was in another world! Suddenly, the instructor waved to me and pointed at his watch. It was difficult to see through my face mask as it is quite old but his signal looked like ten minutes more. I continued swimming around, looking at the fish and rocks and the strange creatures of the sea. Then, suddenly, I started to feel strange - dizzy and tired. There were black spots in front of my eyes and my body was heavy. That is all I remember…

The next thing I remember is I was on the beach, lying on the sand with my instructor. He looked angry.

'What happened?' he said. 'I signalled for you to come to the surface but when I looked back you weren't there. Where were you?'

'You signalled 10 minutes more,' I said. I was still very tired and it was difficult to speak.

'No way,' he said. 'There was fifteen minutes of oxygen in your tank so it was a very short dive. You looked at me, then disappeared. You nearly died. I pulled you to the surface!'

'My mask wasn't clear,' I said. 'It looked like ten minutes to me.'

'I think you need a new mask,' he replied. 'You were very lucky!'

1. Mark wanted to go caving.   **T / F**
2. The mask and fins were his own.   **T / F**
3. The depth gauge shows you how much oxygen is in the tanks. **T / F**
4. The instructor signalled ten minutes more.   **T / F**
5. Mark's instructor was angry with him after the dive.   **T / F**
6. The instructor pulled him to the surface.   **T / F**
7. There was twenty minutes of oxygen in the tank.   **T / F**
8. Mark needs a new mask.   **T / F**

Skills

Listening

2 Listen and circle T (True) or F (False).

1	Mrs Smith worked in a shop.	**T / F**
2	She cleaned a room on the second floor.	**T / F**
3	The director checked on Mrs Smith.	**T / F**
4	The floor was still dirty.	**T / F**
5	Part of the modern sculpture wasn't there.	**T / F**
6	The jacket with five roses wasn't there.	**T / F**
7	The jacket with roses was part of a sculpture.	**T / F**
8	The sculpture was worth £ 40,000.	**T / F**

Writing Letter format

Tip When writing a letter, use 'Dear' at the beginning and 'Love' or 'Best wishes' (if you don't know the person very well) at the end.

 3 Read the letter and circle all the past verbs.

Dear Jo,
I was in Italy for two weeks this year with my family. We stayed for a week in Rome and for a week on the beach near Rome. We visited a lot of famous buildings and museums. I enjoyed it, but I was tired by the end.
The beach was great. I played volleyball and relaxed. I wanted to speak Italian but I didn't. I was too shy!
I loved my holidays.
What about you?
Love,
Pete

4 Reply to Pete's letter and describe your last holiday.

The Story of the Stones 6
Three stones to rule the universe!

Complete the dialogue. Watch Episode 6 again to check.

How dare you!	**Darkman**	It's not the real stone! ....
You're welcome.	**Daniel**	Phew! ....
That was close.	**Sunborn**	Thank you all very much. You were a great help.
	Emma	....

 Go to www.cambridge.org/elt/more for DVD exercises and CYBER HOMEWORK 12b

CLIL History

Biography Modern History Makers

1 Read about Steve Jobs and complete the timeline below.

STEVE JOBS – inventor and businessman

Steve Jobs was born in America in 1955. He was clever and good at electronics, but he dropped out of university. During this time, he did a course in font design. He started the Apple Company in 1976, with his school friend, Steve (Woz) Wozniak, who invented the first Apple computer. Apple computers were more 'user friendly' than other computers. They used images rather than commands – a pair of scissors to show 'Cut', a pen to show 'Colour', etc and clear and easy fonts. He stayed at Apple until 1985 then set up his own company NeXT and bought the animation company Pixar. His company won prizes for *Toy Story* and other films. In 1996, he went back to Apple as the CEO. He died of cancer in 2011.

1955		....	1985	2011
Born	dropped out of uni, course in	Apple formed	set up NeXt	....

2 Read about J.K. Rowling and complete the table below.

J.K. Rowling – author

Jo Rowling was born in England in 1965 and wrote her first story about a rabbit when she was six. She was on a long train journey when she had the ideas for all the Harry Potter books. When she wrote *Harry Potter and the Philosopher's Stone* she was divorced, had a baby girl and no job. She wrote most of the story in cafes in Edinburgh with her daughter asleep in a pushchair! Published in 1997, Harry Potter won the British Children's Book of the Year award. She wrote the next six 'H.P.' books between 1998 and 2007. So far there are more than 450 million copies of Harry Potter books in 72 languages and all the books are now films. Jo Rowling set up the Volant Charitable Trust in 2000. This gives money from her books and films to various charities.

Name:
Born:
Nationality:
Occupation:
History:
Achievements:
Why you think she is special:

WEBQUEST

Find out:
- Who invented the internet and the World Wide Web and why?
- Write a short biography or timeline of this man.

 Go to www.cambridge.org/elt/more for extra **CLIL**

Check your progress 6

1 **Reorder the letters for the names of furniture.**

1 afos ....
2 gdierf ....
3 rahimrac ....
4 pardcbuo ....
5 rahic ....
6 dbseied lbaet ....

☐ **6**

2 **Write the names of the places. [½ point each]**

1 m _ _ _ _ _ _ _   4 r _ _ _ _ _ _ _ _ _
2 t _ _ _ _ _ _   5 t _ _ _ _ p _ _ _
3 a _ _ g _ _ _ _ _ _   6 m _ _ _ _ _

☐ **3**

3 **Complete the sentences.**

1 My brother .... at the museum yesterday. ☑
2 I .... hungry last night. ☒
3 My mum and dad .... at the restaurant on Saturday. ☒
4 We .... at the theme park last month. ☑
5 I .... late for the English lesson. ☑

4 **Match the questions to the answers.**

1 ☐ Was he late for the English lesson?
2 ☐ Were your mum and dad at the theatre?
3 ☐ Was your sister at home on Saturday?
4 ☐ Were we at the party last weekend?
5 ☐ Was I at the art gallery yesterday?

a Yes, I was.   d Yes, they were.
b No, we weren't.   e No, she wasn't.
c Yes, he was.

☐ **5**

5 **Reorder the words to make sentences. Then write the questions. [2 points each]**

1 yesterday / was / at 6 pm / park / My / at / brother / the /.

....

2 Tom's / museum / was / class / the / on Tuesday / at /.

....

3 restaurant / friends / at / My / the / last weekend / were /.

....

4 last night / was / late / She /.

....

5 supermarket / We / on Saturday / the / at / were /.

....

6 I / kitchen / the / was / in /.

....

☐ **12**

6 **Complete the sentences with the Past simple form of the verbs.**

1 They .... on holiday last summer. (relax)
2 We .... computer games all evening. (play)
3 My friends and I .... at the party. (dance)
4 Ben and Dan .... for three hours on Sunday. (walk)
5 My sister .... in London last year. (live)
6 You .... for the bus for 20 minutes. (wait)

☐ **6**

7 **Complete the dialogue.**

A ¹.......................... you at the party on Saturday?
B Yes, I ².......................... .
A ³.......................... Jess there too?
B ⁴ No, she ....
A ⁵.......................... Tom and Ellie there?
B Yes, they ⁶.......................... but Mark and Katie ⁷.......................... there.

☐ **7**

8 **Translate the questions and sentences.**

1 Were you late for school yesterday?

....

2 They weren't at the cinema on Sunday.

....

3 Maria watched TV last night.

....

4 John phoned me last week.

....

5 My cousins stayed at the hotel at the theme park.

....

6 The film finished at 10 pm.

....

☐ **6**

TOTAL ☐ **50**

MY PROGRESS SO FAR IS...   brilliant! ☐   quite good. ☐   not great. ☐

WORDLIST

STARTER

birthday /ˈbɜːθdeɪ/
black /blæk/
blue /bluː/
board /bɔːd/
book /bʊk/
bus /bʌs/
bye /baɪ/
car /kɑː/
chair /tʃeə/
chicken /ˈtʃɪkɪn/
child /tʃaɪld/
colour /ˈkʌlə(r)/
classroom /ˈklɑːsrʊm/
computer /kəmˈpjuːtə(r)/
day /deɪ/
desk /desk/
to do /tə ˈduː/
eight /eɪt/
eighteen /ˌeɪˈtiːn/
eleven /ɪˈlevn/
English /ˈɪŋglɪʃ/
exercise book /ˈeksəsaɪz bʊk/
favourite /ˈfeɪvərɪt/
fifteen /ˌfɪfˈtiːn/
fine /faɪn/
fish /fɪʃ/
five /faɪv/
football /ˈfʊtbɔːl/
food /fuːd/
four /fɔː(r)/
fourteen /ˌfɔːˈtiːn/
Friday /ˈfraɪdeɪ/
friend /frend/
from /frəm/
good afternoon /ˌgʊd ɑːftəˈnuːn/
good evening /ˌgʊd ˈiːvnɪŋ/
good morning /ˌgʊd ˈmɔːnɪŋ/
goodnight /ˌgʊdˈnaɪt/
goodbye /ˌgʊdˈbaɪ/
great /greɪt/
green /griːn/
grey /greɪ/
hamburger /ˈhæmbɜːgə(r)/
hello /həˈləʊ/
hi /haɪ/
homework /ˈhəʊmwɜːk/
hotel /həʊˈtel/
to know /tə ˈnəʊ/
laptop /ˈlæptɒp/
man /mæn/
Monday /ˈmʌndeɪ/
name /neɪm/
nine /naɪn/
nineteen /ˌnaɪnˈtiːn/
number /ˈnʌmbə(r)/
old /əʊld/

one /wʌn/
orange /ˈɒrɪndʒ/
paper /ˈpeɪpə(r)/
pen /pen/
pencil /ˈpensl/
pencil case /ˈpensl keɪs/
person /ˈpɜːsn/
pink /pɪŋk/
pizza /ˈpiːtsə/
purple /ˈpɜːpl/
to read /tə ˈriːd/
red /red/
repeat /rɪˈpiːt/
rubber /ˈrʌbə(r)/
rucksack /ˈrʌksæk/
ruler /ˈruːlə(r)/
Saturday /ˈsætədeɪ/
seven /ˈsevn/
seventeen /ˌsevnˈtiːn/
six /sɪks/
sixteen /ˌsɪksˈtiːn/
student /ˈstjuːdnt/
Sunday /ˈsʌndeɪ/
supermarket /ˈsuːpəmɑːkɪt/
surname /ˈsɜːneɪm/
tablet /ˈtæblət/
taxi /ˈtæksi/
teacher /ˈtiːtʃə(r)/
tell /tel/
ten /ten/
tennis /ˈtenɪs/
thanks /θæŋks/
thirteen /ˌθɜːˈtiːn/
three /θriː/
Thursday /ˈθɜːzdeɪ/
Tuesday /ˈtjuːzdeɪ/
twelve /twelv/
twenty /ˈtwenti/
twenty-one /ˌtwentiˈwʌn/
two /tuː/
understand /ˌʌndəˈstænd/
Wednesday /ˈwenzdeɪ/
week /wiːk/
where /weə(r)/
white /waɪt/
whiteboard /ˈwaɪtbɔːd/
woman /ˈwʊmən/
to work /tə ˈwɜːk/
to write /tə ˈraɪt/
year /yɪə(r)/
yellow /ˈyeləʊ/

UNIT 1

act /ækt/
age /eɪdʒ/
agent /ˈeɪdʒənt/
angry /ˈæŋgri/
area /ˈeəriə/
back /bæk/
band /bænd/

big /bɪg/
biggest /ˈbɪgɪst/
bored /bɔːd/
boy /bɔɪ/
building /ˈbɪldɪŋ/
busy /ˈbɪzi/
capital /ˈkæpɪtl/
capsule /ˈkæpsjuːl/
cat /kæt/
clever /ˈklevə(r)/
clothes /kləʊðz/
cold /kəʊld/
to come /tə ˈkʌm/
copy /ˈkɒpi/
correct /kəˈrekt/
country /ˈkʌntri/
craft /krɑːft/
diary /ˈdaɪəri/
dog /dɒg/
door /dɔː(r)/
England /ˈɪŋglənd/
excited /ɪkˈsaɪtɪd/
famous /ˈfeɪməs/
to feel /tə ˈfiːl/
feeling /ˈfiːlɪŋ/
to go /tə ˈgəʊ/
guest /gest/
happy /ˈhæpi/
here /hɪə(r)/
history /ˈhɪstri/
home /həʊm/
hot /hɒt/
house /haʊs/
hungry /ˈhʌŋgri/
impossible /ɪmˈpɒsəbl/
inside /ˌɪnˈsaɪd/
Ireland /ˈaɪələnd/
Irish /ˈaɪrɪʃ/
language /ˈlæŋgwɪdʒ/
late /leɪt/
look /lʊk/
manager /ˈmænɪdʒə(r)/
market /ˈmɑːkɪt/
maths /mæθs/
meet /miːt/
most /məʊst/
mountain /ˈmaʊntən/
nationality /ˌnæʃəˈnæləti/
nervous /ˈnɜːvəs/
new /njuː/
next /nekst/
nice /naɪs/
of course /əv ˈkɔːs/
party /ˈpɑːti/
PE /ˌpiː ˈiː/
people /ˈpiːpl/
photo /ˈfəʊtəʊ/
place /pleɪs/
police /pəˈliːs/
population /ˌpɒpjəˈleɪʃn/
river /ˈrɪvə(r)/

robber /ˈrɒbə(r)/
robbery /ˈrɒbəri/
roof /ruːf/
round /raʊnd/
royal guard /ˌrɔɪəl ˈgɑːd/
sad /sæd/
same /seɪm/
scared /skeəd/
school /skuːl/
Scotland /ˈskɒtlənd/
servant /ˈsɜːvənt/
shop /ʃɒp/
singer /ˈsɪŋə(r)/
slice /slaɪs/
sorry /ˈsɒri/
stalls /stɔːlz/
sure /ʃʊə(r)/
test /test/
theatre /ˈθɪətə(r)/
tired /ˈtaɪəd/
today /təˈdeɪ/
tomorrow /təˈmɒrəʊ/
very /ˈveri/
Wales /weɪlz/
watch /wɒtʃ/
weekend /ˈwiːkend/
Welsh /welʃ/
wheel /wiːl/
who /huː/
why /waɪ/
worried /ˈwʌrid/

UNIT 2

actor /ˈæktə(r)/
at last /ət ˈlɑːst/
bag /bæg/
behind /bɪˈhaɪnd/
CD player /ˌsiː ˈdiː pleɪə(r)/
chart /tʃɑːt/
to clean /tə ˈkliːn/
to close /tə ˈkləʊz/
corner /ˈkɔːnə(r)/
data /ˈdeɪtə/
eye /aɪ/
Finland /ˈfɪnlənd/
floor /flɔː(r)/
graph /grɑːf/
hair /heə(r)/
headmaster /ˌhedˈmɑːstə(r)/
in /ɪn/
information /ˌɪnfəˈmeɪʃn/
in front of /ɪn ˈfrʌnt əv/
to laugh /tə ˈlɑːf/
to look /tə ˈlʊk/
mat /mæt/
next to /ˈneks tuː/
obviously /ˈɒbviəsli/
on /ɒn/
open /ˈəʊpn/

person (*plural* people) /ˈpɜːsn/ (/ˈpiːpl/)
picture /ˈpɪktʃə(r)/
pie chart /ˈpaɪ tʃɑːt/
poster /ˈpəʊstə(r)/
quiet /ˈkwaɪət/
right /raɪt/
to run /tə ˈrʌn/
to see /tə ˈsiː/
shop /ʃɒp/
to show /tə ˈʃəʊ/
to sit /tə ˈsɪt/
small /smɔːl/
to stand /tə ˈstænd/
strange /streɪndʒ/
to take /tə ˈteɪk/
team /tiːm/
under /ˈʌndə(r)/
window /ˈwɪndəʊ/

UNIT 3

accident /ˈæksɪdənt/
armchair /ˈɑːmtʃeə(r)/
bath /bɑːθ/
bathroom /ˈbɑːθrʊm/
bed /bed/
bedroom /ˈbedrʊm/
bedside table /ˌbedsaɪd ˈteɪbl/
bicycle /ˈbaɪsɪkl/
big /bɪg/
bookcase /ˈbʊkkeɪs/
bookshelf (*plural* bookshelves) /ˈbʊkʃelf/ (/ˈbʊkʃelvz/)
bright /braɪt/
camel /ˈkæml/
camera /ˈkæmərə/
carpet /ˈkɑːpɪt/
children /ˈtʃɪldrən/
comfortable /ˈkʌmftəbl/
cooker /ˈkʊkə(r)/
cow /kaʊ/
cupboard /ˈkʌbəd/
curtain /ˈkɜːtn/
cushion /ˈkʊʃn/
daughter /ˈdɔːtə(r)/
design /dɪˈzaɪn/
DVD player /ˌdiː viː ˈdiː pleɪə(r)/
every /ˈevri/
fantastic /fænˈtæstɪk/
felt /felt/
film /fɪlm/
to float /tə ˈfləʊt/
to fly /tə ˈflaɪ/
frame /freɪm/
fridge /frɪdʒ/
furniture /ˈfɜːnɪtʃə(r)/
garage /ˈgærɑːdʒ/

grass /grɑːs/
to get married /tə ˌget ˈmærid/
hall /hɔːl/
hour /ˈaʊə(r)/
ideal /aɪˈdiːl/
island /ˈaɪlənd/
jacket /ˈdʒækɪt/
joke /dʒəʊk/
kitchen /ˈkɪtʃən/
lake /leɪk/
lamp /læmp/
left /left/
light /laɪt/
living room /ˈlɪvɪŋ rʊm/
long /lɒŋ/
medicine /ˈmedsn/
message /ˈmesɪdʒ/
to miss /tə ˈmɪs/
mobile phone /ˌməʊbaɪl ˈfəʊn/
motor boat /ˈməʊtə bəʊt/
often /ˈɒfn/
pedigree /ˈpedɪgriː/
pig /pɪg/
quickly /ˈkwɪkli/
radio station /ˈreɪdiəʊ steɪʃn/
recycled /ˌriːˈsaɪkld/
reed /riːd/
rug /rʌg/
sheep /ʃiːp/
sink /sɪŋk/
smartphone /ˈsmɑːtfəʊn/
sofa /ˈsəʊfə/
solar panel /ˌsəʊlə ˈpænl/
south /saʊθ/
spell /spel/
steak /steɪk/
stereo /ˈsteriəʊ/
suitcase /ˈsuːtkeɪs/
table /ˈteɪbl/
tea /tiː/
toilet /ˈtɔɪlət/
trophy /ˈtrəʊfi/
unfriendly /ʌnˈfrendli/
wardrobe /ˈwɔːdrəʊb/
washbasin /ˈwɒʃbeɪsn/
whose /huːz/
wood /wʊd/
wooden /ˈwʊdn/
yak /jæk/
yurt /jɜːt/

UNIT 4

accent /ˈæksent/
American /əˈmerɪkən/
Argentina /ˌɑːdʒənˈtiːnə/
Argentinian /ˌɑːdʒənˈtɪniən/
arm /ɑːm/

banana /bəˈnɑːnə/
basketball /ˈbɑːskɪtbɔːl/
beard /bɪəd/
before /bɪˈfɔː(r)/
blonde /blɒnd/
box /bɒks/
Brazil /brəˈzɪl/
Brazilian /brəˈzɪliən/
Britain /ˈbrɪtn/
British /ˈbrɪtɪʃ/
brother /ˈbrʌðə(r)/
butterfly /ˈbʌtəflaɪ/
Canada /ˈkænədə/
Canadian /kəˈneɪdiən/
China /ˈtʃaɪnə/
Chinese /ˌtʃaɪˈniːz/
clue /kluː/
continent /ˈkɒntɪnənt/
curly /ˈkɜːli/
dark /dɑːk/
DVD drive /ˌdiː viː ˈdiː draɪv/
ear /ɪə(r)/
early /ˈɜːli/
equator /ɪˈkweɪtə(r)/
fair /feə(r)/
father /ˈfɑːðə(r)/
feet /fiːt/
finally /ˈfaɪnəli/
finger /ˈfɪŋgə(r)/
flag /flæg/
foot /fʊt/
football player /ˈfʊtbɔːl pleɪə(r)/
France /frɑːns/
French /frentʃ/
Geography /dʒiˈɒgrəfi/
German /ˈdʒɜːmən/
Germany /ˈdʒɜːməni/
glasses /ˈglɑːsɪz/
hair /heə(r)/
hand /hænd/
head /hed/
hook /hʊk/
India /ˈɪndiə/
Indian /ˈɪndiən/
interesting /ˈɪntrəstɪŋ/
Italian /ɪˈtæliən/
Italy /ˈɪtəli/
Jamaica /dʒəˈmeɪkə/
Jamaican /dʒəˈmeɪkən/
Japan /dʒəˈpæn/
Japanese /ˌdʒæpəˈniːz/
leg /leg/
Moroccan /məˈrɒkən/
Morocco /məˈrɒkəʊ/
mountain bike /ˈmaʊntən baɪk/
mouth /maʊθ/
New Zealand /ˌnjuː ˈziːlənd/
New Zealander /ˌnjuː ˈziːləndə(r)/

Nigeria /naɪˈdʒɪəriə/
Nigerian /naɪˈdʒɪəriən/
nose /nəʊz/
parrot /ˈpærət/
pet /pet/
phone /fəʊn/
plump /plʌmp/
shirt /ʃɜːt/
short /ʃɔːt/
shoulder /ˈʃəʊldə(r)/
sister /ˈsɪstə(r)/
slim /slɪm/
Spain /speɪn/
Spanish /ˈspænɪʃ/
sport /spɔːt/
straight /streɪt/
Sweden /ˈswiːdn/
Swedish /ˈswiːdɪʃ/
Swiss /swɪs/
Switzerland /ˈswɪtsələnd/
tall /tɔːl/
teeth /tiːθ/
toe /təʊ/
T-shirt /ˈtiːʃɜːt/
Turkey /ˈtɜːki/
Turkish /ˈtɜːkɪʃ/
umbrella /ʌmˈbrelə/
the USA /ðə ˌjuː es ˈeɪ/
to wear /tə ˈweə(r)/
to worry /tə ˈwʌri/
young /jʌŋ/

UNIT 5

always /ˈɔːlweɪz/
apple /ˈæpl/
athletics /æθˈletɪks/
beans /biːnz/
beef /biːf/
biscuit /ˈbɪskɪt/
boring /ˈbɔːrɪŋ/
bottle /ˈbɒtl/
bread /bred/
breakfast /ˈbrekfəst/
broccoli /ˈbrɒkəli/
bus /bʌs/
butter /ˈbʌtə(r)/
to buy /tə ˈbaɪ/
cake /keɪk/
canteen /kænˈtiːn/
carrot /ˈkærət/
to carry /tə ˈkæri/
to catch /tə ˈkætʃ/
cheeseburger /ˈtʃiːzbɜːgə(r)/
cherry /ˈtʃeri/
chips /tʃɪps/
chocolate /ˈtʃɒklət/
cinema /ˈsɪnəmə/
coffee /ˈkɒfi/

compulsory education
/kəmˌpʌlsəri ˌedʒuˈkeɪʃn/
to cook /tə ˈkʊk/
to cry /tə ˈkraɪ/
cup /kʌp/
curry /ˈkʌri/
delicious /dɪˈlɪʃəs/
dinner /ˈdɪnə(r)/
drink /drɪŋk/
egg /eg/
encourage /ɪnˈkʌrɪdʒ/
expensive /ɪkˈspensɪv/
fee /fiː/
fish /fɪʃ/
fizzy /ˈfɪzi/
fork /fɔːk/
free /friː/
fruit /fruːt/
glass /glɑːs/
grape /greɪp/
to hate /tə ˈheɪt/
healthy /ˈhelθi/
herbal tea /ˌhɜːbl ˈtiː/
hockey /ˈhɒki/
holiday /ˈhɒlɪdeɪ/
ice cream /ˌaɪs ˈkriːm/
to kiss /tə ˈkɪs/
kiwi /ˈkiːwiː/
knife /naɪf/
to leave /tə ˈliːv/
lunch /lʌntʃ/
meal /miːl/
meat /miːt/
milk /mɪlk/
to mix /tə ˈmɪks/
monster /ˈmɒnstə(r)/
month /mʌnθ/
to move /tə ˈmuːv/
mystery /ˈmɪstri/
napkin /ˈnæpkɪn/
never /ˈnevə(r)/
noodle /ˈnuːdl/
to notice /tə ˈnəʊtɪs/
once /wʌns/
onion /ˈʌnjən/
orange /ˈɒrɪndʒ/
orange juice /ˈɒrɪndʒ
ˌdʒuːs/
park /pɑːk/
to pass /tə ˈpɑːs/
plate /pleɪt/
popcorn /ˈpɒpkɔːn/
popular /ˈpɒpjələ(r)/
potato /pəˈteɪtəʊ/
primary school /ˈpraɪməri
skuːl/
pudding /ˈpʊdɪŋ/
quick /kwɪk/
to relax /tə rɪˈlæks/
to remember
/tə rɪˈmembə(r)/

restaurant /ˈrestrɒnt/
rice /raɪs/
rocket /ˈrɒkɪt/
salad /ˈsæləd/
sandwich /ˈsænwɪtʃ/
saucer /ˈsɔːsə(r)/
sausage /ˈsɒsɪdʒ/
sea /siː/
secondary school
/ˈsekəndri skuːl/
ship /ʃɪp/
shopping /ˈʃɒpɪŋ/
sometimes /ˈsʌmtaɪmz/
soup /suːp/
spinach /ˈspɪnɪtʃ/
spoon /spuːn/
to study /tə ˈstʌdi/
submarine /ˌsʌbməˈriːn/
sugar /ˈʃʊgə(r)/
tablecloth /ˈteɪblklɒθ/
tea /tiː/
term /tɜːm/
to tidy /tə ˈtaɪdi/
toast /təʊst/
treasure /ˈtreʒə(r)/
underwater
/ˌʌndəˈwɔːtə(r)/
uniform /ˈjuːnɪfɔːm/
university /juːnəˈvɜːsɪti/
usually /ˈjuːʒəli/
vegetable /ˈvedʒtəbl/
to visit /tə ˈvɪzɪt/
warm /wɔːm/
to wash /tə ˈwɒʃ/
to watch /tə ˈwɒtʃ/
water /ˈwɔːtə(r)/
yoghurt /ˈjɒgət/

UNIT 6

a lot /ə ˈlɒt/
answer /ˈɑːnsə(r)/
away /əˈweɪ/
balanced diet /ˌbælənst
ˈdaɪət/
body /ˈbɒdi/
brother-in-law
/ˈbrʌðərɪnlɔː/
bus stop /ˈbʌs stɒp/
cafeteria /ˌkæfəˈtɪəriə/
carbohydrate
/ˌkɑːbəˈhaɪdreɪt/
cereal /ˈsɪəriəl/
clock /klɒk/
cool /kuːl/
to drive /tə ˈdraɪv/
end /end/
energy /ˈenədʒi/
expensive /ɪkˈspensɪv/
to explain /tu ɪkˈspleɪn/
farm /fɑːm/

fat /fæt/
to feed /tə ˈfiːd/
fibre /ˈfaɪbə(r)/
to finish /tə ˈfɪnɪʃ/
first /fɜːst/
fishing /ˈfɪʃɪŋ/
fuel /ˈfjuːəl/
fun /fʌn/
genetically modified food
/dʒəˌnetɪkli ˌmɒdɪfaɪd
ˈfuːd/
to get up /tə ˌget ˈʌp/
to give /tə ˈgɪv/
to hand out /tə ˌhænd ˈaʊt/
hard /hɑːd/
to have breakfast /tə ˌhæv
ˈbrekfəst/
horse /hɔːs/
ill /ɪl/
instrument /ˈɪnstrəmənt/
to interview /tu ˈɪntəvjuː/
life /laɪf/
to listen to /tə ˈlɪsn tuː/
to live /tə ˈlɪv/
to make fun of /tə ˌmeɪk
ˈfʌn əv/
mineral /ˈmɪnərəl/
money /ˈmʌni/
mother /ˈmʌðə(r)/
music /ˈmjuːzɪk/
northern /ˈnɔːðən/
o'clock /əˈklɒk/
oh dear /ˌəʊ ˈdɪə(r)/
oil /ɔɪl/
parent /ˈpeərənt/
piano /piˈænəʊ/
to play /tə ˈpleɪ/
to practise /tə ˈpræktɪs/
protein /ˈprəʊtiːn/
to repair /tə rɪˈpeə(r)/
to ride a horse /tə ˌraɪd ə
ˈhɔːs/
rollerblading
/ˈrəʊləbleɪdɪŋ/
routine /ruːˈtiːn/
to send /tə ˈsend/
to snore /tə ˈsnɔː(r)/
to speak /tə ˈspiːk/
specific /spəˈsɪfɪk/
to spend /tə ˈspend/
sports centre /ˈspɔːts
sentə(r)/
to start /tə ˈstɑːt/
to surf /tə ˈsɜːf/
Sunday /ˈsʌndeɪ/
sweets /swiːts/
to talk /tə ˈtɔːk/
thing /θɪŋ/
Thursday /ˈθɜːzdeɪ/
trainer /ˈtreɪnə(r)/
vitamin /ˈvɪtəmɪn/

to wake up /tə ˌweɪk ˈʌp/
to walk /tə ˈwɔːk/
to want /tə ˈwɒnt/
way /weɪ/

UNIT 7

to argue /tu ˈɑːgjuː/
balloon /bəˈluːn/
to bat /tə ˈbæt/
to bowl /tə ˈbəʊl/
cap /kæp/
card /kɑːd/
casual /ˈkæʒuəl/
clothes /kləʊðz/
coach /kəʊtʃ/
confused /kənˈfjuːzd/
denim /ˈdenɪm/
document /ˈdɒkjəmənt/
dress /dres/
to dribble /tə ˈdrɪbl/
excuse me /ɪkˈskjuːz miː/
family /ˈfæməli/
goal /gəʊl/
goose (plural geese) /guːs/
(/giːs/)
guitar /gɪˈtɑː(r)/
gym /dʒɪm/
hairband /ˈheəbænd/
ham /hæm/
hat /hæt/
hen /hen/
to hold on /tə ˌhəʊld ˈɒn/
hole /həʊl/
hood /hʊd/
how many /ˌhaʊ ˈmeni/
how much /ˌhaʊ ˈmʌtʃ/
jeans /dʒiːnz/
key-ring /ˈkiːrɪŋ/
to lend /tə ˈlend/
magazine /ˌmægəˈziːn/
match /mætʃ/
messy /ˈmesi/
nail /neɪl/
MP3 player /ˌem piː ˈtriː
pleɪə(r)/
to paint /tə ˈpeɪnt/
pair /peə(r)/
pocket /ˈpɒkɪt/
present /ˈpreznt/
price /praɪs/
problem /ˈprɒbləm/
ready /ˈredi/
ring /rɪŋ/
sandal /ˈsændl/
to score /tə ˈskɔː(r)/
shoe /ʃuː/
skirt /skɜːt/
smart /smɑːt/
to smile /tə ˈsmaɪl/
sock /sɒk/

spotted /ˈspɒtɪd/
stick /stɪk/
striker /ˈstraɪkə(r)/
sweater /ˈswetə(r)/
to tackle /tə ˈtækl/
top /tɒp/
tournament /ˈtɔːnəmənt/
to train /tə ˈtreɪn/
trousers /ˈtraʊzəz/
to try on /tə ˌtraɪ ˈɒn/
volleyball /ˈvɒlibɔːl/
warm-up /ˈwɔːmʌp/
to win /tə ˈwɪn/

UNIT 8

acrobat /ˈækrəbæt/
alphabet /ˈælfəbet/
aunt /ɑːnt/
bell /bel/
to borrow /tə ˈbɒrəʊ/
cello /ˈtʃeləʊ/
clarinet /ˌklærəˈnet/
to climb /tə ˈklaɪm/
cousin /ˈkʌzn/
cymbal /ˈsɪmbl/
to dance /tə ˈdɑːns/
difficult /ˈdɪfɪkəlt/
to dive /tə ˈdaɪv/
drum /drʌm/
exercise /ˈeksəsaɪz/
father-in-law /ˈfɑːðərɪnlɔː/
fit /fɪt/
flute /fluːt/
gong /gɒŋ/
grandfather /ˈgrænfɑːðə(r)/
grandmother /ˈgrænmʌðə(r)/
grandparent /ˈgrænpeərənt/
Greek /griːk/
harp /hɑːp/
harpsichord /ˈhɑːpsɪkɔːd/
hear /hɪə(r)/
hippo /ˈhɪpəʊ/
horn /hɔːn/
ice skating /ˈaɪs skeɪtɪŋ/
instrument /ˈɪnstrəmənt/
to juggle /tə ˈdʒʌgl/
kilometre /ˈkɪləmiːtə(r)/
length /leŋθ/
luck /lʌk/
lucky /ˈlʌki/
moment /ˈməʊmənt/
mother-in-law /ˈmʌðərɪnlɔː/
oboe /ˈəʊbəʊ/
opera /ˈɒprə/
orchestra /ˈɔːkestrə/
pool /puːl/
recorder /rɪˈkɔːdə(r)/
to roller blade /tə ˈrəʊlə bleɪd/

row /rəʊ/
safety net /ˈseɪfti net/
saxophone /ˈsæksəfəʊn/
show /ʃəʊ/
shower /ˈʃaʊə(r)/
to sing /tə ˈsɪŋ/
skiing /ˈskiːɪŋ/
surprise /səˈpraɪz/
to swim /tə ˈswɪm/
tambourine /ˌtæmbəˈriːn/
tightrope-walking /ˈtaɪtrəʊpwɔːkɪŋ/
tonight /təˈnaɪt/
tree /triː/
triangle /ˈtraɪæŋgl/
trombone /trɒmˈbəʊn/
trumpet /ˈtrʌmpɪt/
tuba /ˈtjuːbə/
uncle /ˈʌŋkl/
to unicycle /tə ˈjuːnɪsaɪkl/
violin /ˌvaɪəˈlɪn/

UNIT 9

advertisement /ædˈvɜːtɪsmənt/
air /eə(r)/
April /ˈeɪprəl/
August /ˈɔːgəst/
to calculate /tə ˈkælkjuleɪt/
to call /tə ˈkɔːl/
to celebrate /tə ˈselɪbreɪt/
credit /ˈkredɪt/
December /dɪˈsembə(r)/
to disturb /tə dɪˈstɜːb/
eighth /eɪtθ/
embarrassing /ɪmˈbærəsɪŋ/
to enjoy /tu ɪnˈdʒɔɪ/
essay /ˈeseɪ/
event /ɪˈvent/
fan /fæn/
February /ˈfebruəri/
fifth /fɪfθ/
formula /ˈfɔːmjələ/
Hallowe'en /ˌhæləʊˈiːn/
to happen /tə ˈhæpn/
information /ˌɪnfəˈmeɪʃn/
to invent /tu ɪnˈvent/
invention /ɪnˈvenʃn/
January /ˈdʒænjuəri/
July /dʒuˈlaɪ/
June /dʒuːn/
to look after /tə ˌlʊk ˈɑːftə(r)/
marathon /ˈmærəθən/
March /mɑːtʃ/
May /meɪ/
newspaper /ˈnjuːzpeɪpə(r)/
November /nəˈvembə(r)/
October /ɒkˈtəʊbə(r)/
outside /ˌaʊtˈsaɪd/
pastime /ˈpɑːstaɪm/

phone number /ˈfəʊn nʌmbə(r)/
policeman /pəˈliːsmən/
police station /pəˈliːs steɪʃn/
potion /ˈpəʊʃn/
probably /ˈprɒbəbli/
programme /ˈprəʊgræm/
to record /tə rɪˈkɔːd/
second /ˈsekənd/
security guard /sɪˈkjʊərəti gɑːd/
September /sepˈtembə(r)/
shopping centre /ˈʃɒpɪŋ sentə(r)/
skateboard /ˈskeɪtbɔːd/
to snow /tə ˈsnəʊ/
soap opera /ˈsəʊp ɒprə/
soon /suːn/
stadium /ˈsteɪdiəm/
strong /strɒŋ/
teen /tiːn/
terrible /ˈterɪbl/
text message /ˈtekst mesɪdʒ/
theme /θiːm/
thief /θiːf/
third /θɜːd/
toy /tɔɪ/
to travel /tə ˈtrævl/
TV presenter /ˌtiː ˈviː prɪzentə(r)/
twelfth /twelfθ/
you're welcome /jə ˈwelkəm/

UNIT 10

art /ɑːt/
backup /ˈbækʌp/
beautiful /ˈbjuːtɪfl/
blog /blɒg/
bracelet /ˈbreɪslət/
to burn /tə ˈbɜːn/
cable /ˈkeɪbl/
charity /ˈtʃærəti/
to check /tə ˈtʃek/
to check out /tə ˌtʃek ˈaʊt/
chemical /ˈkemɪkl/
to click /tə ˈklɪk/
to collect /tə kəˈlekt/
to connect /tə kəˈnekt/
to create /tə kriˈeɪt/
to download /tə ˌdaʊnˈləʊd/
drawer /drɔː(r)/
file /faɪl/
to fill up /tə ˌfɪl ˈʌp/
to fix /tə ˈfɪks/
free time /ˌfriː ˈtaɪm/
graffiti /grəˈfiːti/
hard disk /ˌhɑːd ˈdɪsk/

to interview /tu ˈɪntəvjuː/
invitation /ˌɪnvɪˈteɪʃn/
landfill /ˈlændfɪl/
link /lɪŋk/
lost /lɒst/
mouse /maʊs/
mug /mʌg/
opposite /ˈɒpəzɪt/
owl /aʊl/
to print /tə ˈprɪnt/
printer /ˈprɪntə(r)/
program /ˈprəʊgræm/
rich /rɪtʃ/
secret /ˈsiːkrət/
software /ˈsɒftweə(r)/
square /skweə(r)/
trap /træp/
to upload /tu ˌʌpˈləʊd/
virus /ˈvaɪrəs/
wrong /rɒŋ/
zebra /ˈzebrə/

UNIT 11

above /əˈbʌv/
ago /əˈgəʊ/
to arrest /tu əˈrest/
attack /əˈtæk/
to believe /tə bɪˈliːv/
between /bɪˈtwiːn/
brilliant /ˈbrɪliənt/
butler /ˈbʌtlə(r)/
ceremony /ˈserəməni/
cook /kʊk/
to date /tə ˈdeɪt/
to drill /tə ˈdrɪl/
expert /ˈekspɜːt/
to fail /tə ˈfeɪl/
footprint /ˈfʊtprɪnt/
to found /tə ˈfaʊnd/
human /ˈhjuːmən/
lamp /læmp/
landmark /ˈlændmɑːk/
library /ˈlaɪbrəri/
maid /meɪd/
play /pleɪ/
to scare /tə ˈskeə(r)/
sick /sɪk/
to stay /tə ˈsteɪ/
tourist /ˈtʊərɪst/
tower /ˈtaʊə(r)/
typical /ˈtɪpɪkl/
truth /truːθ/
village /ˈvɪlɪdʒ/
yesterday /ˈjestədeɪ/

UNIT 12

amazing /əˈmeɪzɪŋ/
art gallery /ˈɑːt gæləri/
aqualung /ˈækwəlʌŋ/

to arrive /tu əˈraɪv/
baby /ˈbeɪbi/
backpack /ˈbækpæk/
to book /tə ˈbʊk/
boot /buːt/
café /ˈkæfeɪ/
to camp /tə ˈkæmp/
camping /ˈkæmpɪŋ/
campsite /ˈkæmpsaɪt/
cancer /ˈkænsə(r)/
caving /ˈkeɪvɪŋ/
to chase /tə ˈtʃeɪs/
church /tʃɜːtʃ/
clear /klɪə(r)/
to cut /tə ˈkʌt/
to die /tə ˈdaɪ/
director /daɪˈrektə(r)/
dizzy /ˈdɪzi/
to drop out /tə ˌdrɒp ˈaʊt/
electronics /ɪˌlekˈtrɒnɪks/
exhibition /ˌeksɪˈbɪʃn/
festival /ˈfestɪvl/
fin /fɪn/
font /fɒnt/
form /fɔːm/
heavy /ˈhevi/
helmet /ˈhelmɪt/
helpful /ˈhelpfl/
hiking /ˈhaɪkɪŋ/
hostel /ˈhɒstl/
to hurry /tə ˈhʌri/
instructor /ɪnˈstrʌktə(r)/
job /dʒɒb/
to jump /tə ˈdʒʌmp/
kayak /ˈkaɪæk/
kayaking /ˈkaɪækɪŋ/
mask /mɑːsk/
monument /ˈmɒnjumənt/
museum /mjuːˈziəm/
paddle /ˈpædl/
prize /praɪz/
pushchair /ˈpʊʃtʃeə(r)/
rabbit /ˈræbɪt/
to rain /tə ˈreɪn/
to reply /tə rɪˈplaɪ/
to rescue /tə ˈreskjuː/
to ring /tə ˈrɪŋ/
rock /rɒk/
rope /rəʊp/
rose /rəʊz/
rubbish /ˈrʌbɪʃ/
scissors /ˈsɪzəz/
scuba diving /ˈskuːbə daɪvɪŋ/
sculpture /ˈskʌlptʃə(r)/
to shout /tə ˈʃaʊt/
to signal /tə ˈsɪgnəl/
to sleep /tə ˈsliːp/
sleeping bag /ˈsliːpɪŋ bæg/
snorkel /ˈsnɔːkl/
snorkelling /ˈsnɔːkəlɪŋ/

special /ˈspeʃl/
sunny /ˈsʌni/
surface /ˈsɜːfɪs/
swimming costume /ˈswɪmɪŋ kɒstjuːm/
swimming pool /ˈswɪmɪŋ puːl/
tank /tæŋk/
tent /tent/
theme park /ˈθiːm pɑːk/
to touch /tə ˈtʌtʃ/
train /treɪn/
weather /ˈweðə(r)/
wetsuit /ˈwetsuːt/

PRONUNCIATION GUIDE

Vowels

/iː/	see
/ɪ/	bit
/e/	bed
/æ/	sad
/ɑː/	father
/ʌ/	cut
/ʊ/	cook
/uː/	too
/i/	happy
/ə/	above
/ɒ/	got
/ɔː/	saw
/u/	actual

Diphthongs

/ɜː/	circle
/eɪ/	say
/aɪ/	buy
/ɔɪ/	boy
/əʊ/	go
/aʊ/	now
/ɪə/	hear
/eə/	hair
/ʊə/	sure
/juː/	few
/aɪə/	fire
/aʊə/	power

Consonants

/p/	push		/ʒ/	measure
/b/	bank		/h/	hot
/t/	time		/w/	water
/d/	diary		/tʃ/	chair
/k/	carpet		/dʒ/	joke
/g/	big		/m/	more
/f/	surf		/n/	snow
/v/	very		/ŋ/	sing
/θ/	thin		/r/	ring
/ð/	that		/l/	small
/s/	sit		/j/	you
/z/	zero			
/ʃ/	shine			

IRREGULAR VERB LIST

Present	Past		Present	Past
become	became		leave	left
begin	began		lose	lost
break	broke		make	made
build	built		meet	met
buy	bought		put	put
come	came		read	read
cut	cut		ring	rang
dig	dug		run	ran
do	did		say	said
drive	drove		see	saw
fall	fell		sing	sang
fight	fought		sit	sat
find	found		sleep	slept
fly	flew		speak	spoke
forget	forgot		stand	stood
get	got		steal	stole
get up	got up		take	took
give	gave		take off	took off
go	went		teach	taught
have	had		tell	told
hear	heard		think	thought
hit	hit		wake	woke
hold	held		win	won
know	knew		write	wrote

CAMBRIDGE

PRACTICE
for your
GRAMMAR!

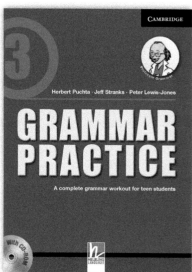

Grammar Practice is a series of four books, recommended for use with MORE! 2nd edition, that help students from age 9 upwards to explore, understand and practise grammar from beginner to intermediate level (A1 – B1) in situational and meaningful contexts.

- Clear **grammar overviews** and rules

- A wide range of productive and receptive **grammar exercises**

- **Interactive CD-ROM** featuring Professor Grammar and his friend, the robot

communication made easy | HELBLING LANGUAGES | www.helblinglanguages.com

CAMBRIDGE UNIVERSITY PRESS
www.cambridge.org/elt

HELBLING LANGUAGES
www.helblinglanguages.com

MORE! 2nd Edition Student's Book 1
by Herbert Puchta & Jeff Stranks with G. Gerngross, C. Holzmann, P. Lewis Jones

First published 2014

20 19 18 17 16 15 14

Printed in Great Britain by CPI Group (UK) Ltd, Croydon CR0 4YY

A catalogue record for this book is available from the British Library
ISBN 9781107656451 MORE! 2nd Edition Student's Book 1
ISBN 9781107681354 MORE! 2nd Edition Workbook 1
ISBN 9781107689695 MORE! 2nd Edition Teacher's Book 1
ISBN 9781107691551 MORE! 2nd Edition Audio Set 1 (3 CDs)
ISBN 9781107652743 MORE! 2nd Edition Testbuilder CD-ROM 1
ISBN 9781107652057 MORE! 2nd Edition Presentation Plus DVD-ROM 1
ISBN 9781107671270 MORE! 2nd Edition *The Story of the Stones* DVD 1

The authors would like to thank:
Oonagh Wade and Rosamund Cantalamessa for their expertise in working on the manuscripts, their useful suggestions for improvement, and the support we got from them.
Lucia Astuti and Markus Spielmann, Helbling Languages, Frances Lowndes and James Dingle, Cambridge University Press, for their dedication to the project and innovative publishing vision.
Our designers, Amanda Hockin, Greg Sweetnam, Barbara Prentiss and the team at Pixarte for their imaginative layouts. Also, our art editor, Francesca Gironi, for her dedicated work.

The publishers would like to thank the following for their kind permission to reproduce the following photographs and other copyright material:
Action Plus Sports Images **/ Alamy** p45 (Jessica Ennis; Dong Dong); Ron Chapple p7 (girl), Monkey Business Images p7 (boy), Christian Delbert p8 (Ferrari), Ron Chapple p8 (girl), Gualtiero Boffi p8 (teacher), Dmitriy Shironosov p8 (teen friends), Joseandres27 p10 (Ronaldo), Sbukley p10 (Mila Kunis; Robert Pattinson and Kristen Stewart), Edward Fielding p10 (Batmobile), Tracy Whiteside p11 (girl), Stephen Coburn p12 (taxi), Effe45 p12 (pizza), Pavel Losevsky p12 (bus), Micka p12 (supermarket), Lightkeeper p12 (football), Johnfoto p12 (hamburger), Jun Mu p12 (hotel), Alexstar p12 (tennis racket), Ingvar Bjork p12 (hotel), Monkey Business Images p13 (Sarah), Bjørn Hovdal p22 (London Eye), Marina Dyakonova p25 (boy), Anke Van Wyk p30 (schoolbus), Serrnovik p31 (blonde girl), Andreykuzmin p31 (ruler), Rafal Glebowski p35 (car), James Boudreaux p35 (laptop), Dan Breckwoldt p42 (The floating village of Uros), Vasilis Ververidis p45 (Usain Bolt), Cammeraydave p47 (laptop), Daniele Taurino p47 (iPad), Photographerlondon p49 (girl), Monkey Business Images p49 (boy), Pioneer111 p60 (French fries), Paul Simcock p61 (Sarah), Anke Van Wyk p62 (Hockey), Andres Rodriguez p62 (college students), Crazy80frog p70 (Bradley), Photographerlondon p70 (girl playing piano), Hongqi Zhang (aka Michael Zhang) p71, Brandon Alms p75 (dvd), Africa Studio p75 (T-shirt), Yobro10 p77 (girl), Eugene Shapovalov p77 (girl, exercise 5), Amy S. Myers p82 (Diane), Davetroesh p82 (Emma), Elena Elisseeva p85 (girl riding horse), 3quarks p90 (acrobat with silk), Lightpoet p90 (teenager ice skating), Timurpix p91, Wavebreakmedia Ltd p95 (girl on mobile phone), Jorg Hackemann p95 (boy on mobile phone), Suzanne Tucker p97 (boy), Godfer p99, Yurchyk p101 (Caroline), Karelnoppe p101 (Jude), Alinso p102 (Tracy), Jacek Chabraszewski p105 (two students talking in park), Noam Armonn p106 (woman walking), Peter Muzslay p106 (teenagers playing soccer), Sian Cox p109 (Janice), Endostock p109 (Joe), Zoom-zoom p110 (graffiti), Dean Bertoncelj p110 (key rings), Ulrich Willmünder p110 (snow owl), Iuliia Kovalova p115 (cinema), Aprescindere p115 (bus stop), Alexandre Zveiger p115 (gym), Filipe Varela p116 (refrigerator), Zoryen p116 (sink), Anton Starikov p116 (radiator), Anastasia Tsoupa p116 (bed), Michaelfair p116 (sofa), Wisconsinart p116 (table), Maxim Kostenko p116 (armchair), Alexander Morozov p116 (curtain), Benis Arapovic p116 (chair), Edgaras Kurauskas p116 (bedside table), Rene Waerts p122 (Hadrian's wall), Martin Brayley p124 (Bestival, Isle of Wight), Elena Stepanova p125 (girl), John Casey p126 (snorkeling), Lupoalb68 p126 (show), Indos82 p126 (monument), Luigi Roscia p126 (art gallery), Cameramannz p126 (theatre), Galyna Andrushko p126 (hiking), Elnur p126 (restaurant), Hongqi Zhang (aka Michael Zhang) p131, Sbukley p132 (JK Rowling) I **Dreamstime.com; ©IStockphoto.com/** Blue_Cutler p6 (girls talking), spfoto p8, jane p17 (Mike), track5 p15 (students in uniform), KeithBinns p17 (Jane), spfoto p17 (Jackie), Fly_Fast p17 (Tom), gbh007 p25 (girl), VikramRaghuvanshi p30 (school in India), BRPH p30 (empty classroom), LindaYolanda p31 (Emma), pepifoto p31 (pencil case), buzbuzzer p35 (block of flat), Livinglmages p37 (boy), JenniferPhotographyImaging p37 (girl), ktaylorg p39 (Meg), JBryson p39 (Sarah), asiseeit p39 (Ben), JBryson p39 (Sue), jane p40 (girl), jabejon p40 (boy), stray_cat p41, robas p42 (house in Vietnam), jonya p51 (boy), kaczka p51 (girl), ArtisticCaptures p61 (Ben), Brosa p61 (Chris), monkeybusinessimages p62 (students in the Cafeteria), pictafolio p75 (magazines), LoooZaaa p75 (computer game), inakiantonana p76 (woman), nakiantonana p76 (smart), Brosa p77 (boy), 3bugsmom p77 (afro American boy), leisadavis p82 (boy playing cricket), Nobilior p85 (girl driving car), Zhenikeyev p85 (telling jokes), izusek (teens talking), STEEX p85 (grandfather), keithferrisphoto p85 (aunt), spfoto p85 (Ben), rhyman007 p90 (horse riding), Jimak p90 (soccer), lisegagne p97 (girl), BirdofPrey p97 (skateboarding), Lisa-Blue p102 (girl watching tv), miljko p106 (swimming), damircudic p106 (meet friends), webphotographeer p106 (bike ride), Dizzo p106 (skateboarding), shironosov p106 (jogging), Serega p108, SlowRunning p109 (Mike), jimbycat p109 (Ted), leisadavis p109 (Jake and Tim), huronphoto p110 (Mark), asiseeit p110 (Grace), EHStock p110 (Sarah), Squaredpixels p115 (shopping); Lisa F. Young p6 (Ahmed, Matt), sianc p8 (boy with hat), Jacek Chabraszewski p8 (students talking), Anna Merzlyakova p8 (notebooks), Max Topchii p11 (boy), Sergey Novikov p13 (Jake), oliveromg p13 (Michael), sianc p13 (Alice), Diego Cervo p15 (students outdoors), Felix Mizioznikov p17 (Simon), Jaimie Duplass p17 (Erica), SergiyN p21, Lance Bellers p22 (Globe Theatre), r.nagy p22 (Buckingham Palace), Tupungato p22 (Covent Garden), Paul Matthew Photography p30 (Catalina), Arvind Balaraman p30 (Alhad), Tracy Whiteside p30 (Arro), oliveromg p31 (boy), Mike Flippo p31 (backpack), Kolobrod p35 (bedroom), Artazum and Iriana Shiyan p38, MANDY GODBEHEAR p39 (Noel), Suzanne Tucker p39 (David), withGod p42 (Mongolian houses), InnaFelker p42 (The Ndebele women), Neale Cousland p45 (Bernard Tomic), Diego Barbieri p45 (Elisa Di Francisca), Mitch Gunn p45 (Michael Phelps), Goodluz p50, BigRoloImages p51, Joana Lopes p55 (teenage girl), Indigo Fish p55 (boy), Nattika p60 (fork), Monkey Business Images p60 (Fish pie), spaxiax p60 (salad), Sarah2 p60 (toast), Sergio33 p60 (chocolate cake), Monkey Business Images p62 (students in uniform), Johnny Photo p65, AlexRoz p67, Bplanet p70 (fish), 6493866629 p75 (dog food), Maxx-Studio p75 (mobile phone), Jessmine p75 (MP3 player), Bayanova Svetlana p75 (key), Redshinestudio p75 (CD), Brian A Jackson p75 (sweets), Elnur sint p75 (blue jeans), Rose Carson p75 (book), p76 (boy), Franck Boston p85 (girl playing guitar), cozyta p85 (boy with camera), Ambrophoto p86 (grandmother), Goodluz p86 (uncle; mother; father), Monkey Business Images p86 (cousin), Igor Bulgarin p90 (circus artist on hoop), IM_photo p90 (skier), Tumar p90 (rollerblading), Andrey Yurlov p90 (swimmer), Andrey Shadrin p90 (teenager with laptop), Andrey Shadrin p95 (boy with laptop on mobile phone), Accord p100 (boy texting), Monkey Business Images p100 (Cheryl), S.Borisov p101 (Colosseum), Tracy Whiteside p102 (Tracy), Christine Langer-Pueschel p105, Kitch Bain p106 (computer), Yeko Photo Studio p106 (woman exercising), Gladskikh Tatiana p106 (teenagers having ice cream), Monkey Business Images p106 (teenagers having pizza), Zurijeta p106 (woman walking the dog), Alexey Fursov p106 (boy rollerblading), Jacek Chabraszewski p109 (Jill and Tessa), Kati Neudert p111, Peteri p115 (London train station), Peter Radacsi p115 (park), Pressmaster p115 (teenage friends), terekhov igor p116 (wardrobe), OZaiachin p116 (cooker), Slobodan Babic p116 (cupboard), Africa Studio p116 (carpet), Melkerw p116 (rug), FrameAngel p116 (lamp), Phase4Studios p122 (Stonehenge), jorisvo p122 (Stratford upon Avon), Elena Elisseeva p122 (Houses of Parliament), Edyta Pawlowska p122 (students), Max Topchii p125 (boy), Jacek Chabraszewski p126 (biking), wavebreakmedia p126 (camping), Jarous p126 (climbers), Rich Carey p126 (scuba diving), salajean p126 (caving), Oleg Zabielin p126 (kayaker), schantalao p126 (theme park), Bikeworldtravel p126 (museum), straga p126 (river), Rich Carey p130, Featureflash p132 (Steve Jobs) **/Shutterstock.com; Wikimedia Commons** Deutsch, Otto Erich p92 (Barbara Krafft's portrait of Mozart).

Commissioned Photography & Production by Matt Devitt & Charlotte Macpherson pp 14, 15, 24, 34, 44, 54, 64, 74, 84, 94, 104, 114, 124.
Story of the Stones by Toonz Animation.

Illustrated by Roberto Battestini, Michela Caputo, Oscar Celestini, Giovanni Giorgi Pierfranceschi, Silvia Provantini, Lorenzo Sabbatini, Giulia Sagramola, Marzia Sanfilippo, Lucilla Stellato.

Every effort has been made to trace the owners of any copyright material in this book. If notified, the publishers will be pleased to rectify any errors or omissions.